GRACE
Like RAIN

GRACE *Like* RAIN

Dr. C. Faith Fredrick

Faith Christian University Press

Faith Christian University Press
210 N. Bumby
Orlando, FL 32803
407-896-6211

Printed in the United States of America

ISBN: 0-9786784-0-0

**For booking information visit
www.FaithFredrick.com**

DEDICATION

This book is lovingly dedicated to:

Bud Fredrick,
my husband, knight in shining armor,
and partner in the Faith.
Thank you for introducing me to the reality
of a vibrant life, full of faith and hope.
Thank you for your wisdom, integrity
and genuineness.
You are one in a million!

CONTENTS

ACKNOWLEDGMENTS

This book would not be possible
without the love and support of ...

My wonderful mother, Dorothy Arnold,
who never compromised but stood strong to teach,
train and be an example of the grace of God.

My children and grandchildren who serve
to be a never-ending inspiration to me:
Marvelyne Adams:
Taylor, Jordan and Maddison
Mary & Steve Alessi:
Christopher, Stephanie, Lauren & Gabrielle
Martha & Dan Munizzi:
Danielle, Nicole & Nathan

I am grateful to my daughter Marvelyne,
for bringing her gifts and talents to this book.
Her editing expertise brought balance, insight
and sound advice to keep us moving in the right
direction. *Thank you for seeing what I saw.*

All the staff, students, alumni and friends of
Faith Christian University.

FOREWORD

"**H**it the ground running!" My mother so confidently said to me as I was walking through one of the toughest transitions of my life. "Don't look back, don't waste time holding on to hurts." My husband and I were at a crossroad of decision; struggling with rejection, unforgiveness and disillusionment. I wanted to hear comfort, not necessarily advice. But my mother knew all too well the danger of focusing on the past. I had to heed her words carefully because I knew the nightmare she survived. I was there. I witnessed her overcome heartbreak, and use it as a stepping stone to more anointing, more understanding … and a new depth of grace.

No one is as tenacious, strong willed, and positive as my mother, Faith Fredrick. After reading her story, you'll know what I'm talking about. Her steadfast resolve and determination to conquer, despite the odds, has always been an incredible example to me.

This is a story of a woman whose faith was tested through the pain of a very difficult divorce. My sisters and I watched our mother go from a place of despair to a place of destiny.

This book will help you discover the real revelation of "God's Grace." It will change the way you look at forgiveness. It will awaken you to a greater understanding of the blessing God has provided for you. It will give you insight into the role we have in experiencing grace for our own lives, as well as ministering grace to others.

As a 16 year old girl, I watched as my mom was stripped of her marriage, her joy, and ultimately what she thought was her purpose. Now, as a woman, I've watched God give her everything back, and so much more; a man that loves her, a successful and fulfilling ministry and a new destiny.

I thank God for my mother. I wouldn't be who I am today without her. I wouldn't have the strength to do what I do. Her revelation of grace changed my life – and it's about to change yours.

Martha Munizzi
Recording Artist / Songwriter

CHAPTER 1

My Journey of Grace

Tears stung my eyes as I opened the envelope. A wave of coldness swept over me. Carefully unfolding the document, I began reading the words that would forever change my life. Here was the judgment in black and white. Despite all of my efforts this document that I held in my hand was a formal decree from a judge and it read, *Divorce Granted*. I could do nothing to change it. This wasn't the way my journey was supposed to unfold. My life had been spent serving God and loving my family; I had been a pastor's wife and mother, devoted to ministry.

Growing up in the 50's, my small town life was a lot like the television program *Happy Days* with a Christian twist. Our world revolved around family and church and our expectations were somewhat simple. One of my favorite childhood memories is Easter. My mother always made my sister and me very beautiful dresses with lots of lace, and we wore sparkling white patent baby doll shoes. Our accessories included white frilly socks, little white lace gloves, and of course an Easter bonnet! I can still see the church platform surrounded with white Easter lilies and the wooden cross that hung on the wall draped in purple satin. The spirit of Easter Sunday was complete when the small congregation stood to sing *"Up from the grave He arose, with a mighty triumph o're His foes."*

By the time I was three years old I was playing 'pretend' piano on everything: coffee tables, backs of church pews, kitchen countertops, every flat surface available. Anytime someone musical came to our church I would sit mesmerized by every move they made. My mother recognized my passion and began to cultivate my talent. I started piano lessons at age nine and within a short time I was playing the piano in children's church. It became my life! If my hands were not physically on the piano keys my mind was visualizing each note and chord. In those days, drums and guitars were considered out of place in the church but pianos and organs were acceptable, so I began to master the piano and eventually took on the challenge of the organ.

I can remember going to the church during the summertime and practicing hour after hour with no air conditioning. The temperatures would often reach 100 degrees, but it didn't matter to me! In my mind, I was in a world of my own, ministering to thousands. Perspiration poured off me as I played and sang every gospel song I had ever heard!

Over the years dynamic pastors, missionaries and evangelists came and went from our little church and

I would sit like a sponge, soaking up everything. My mother made sure that our home was always open to special guests from the church and a feast was in store for everyone at our table.

There weren't many activities in our tiny southern area, so nearly everyone looked forward to the tent revivals that would come through. The evangelist was always fiery and the music amazing. My heart was smitten with the desire to duplicate what I was hearing. The tent was hot and sticky with plenty of dust and dirt, but it was exciting. You never knew who would walk under the canopy of that brown fabric sanctuary or stand in the darkness hoping to go unnoticed. Many would drive up, roll down their windows – and simply listen.

Following a soul-stirring message, the musicians and singers would come take their places and the preacher would make an appeal for people to give their lives to Christ. Men and women, boys and girls would come with tears streaming down their faces to the makeshift altars. Many times a head would peer out from the darkness and duck under the canopy of the tent to be beckoned forward to accept Christ. Maybe it was someone that had been labeled "the towns' hopeless case" or some Godly mother's son drawn by her prayers. It was not unusual that you would hear a car door open in the distance and you would wait in anticipation to see who had driven up as a spectator and now been quickened by the Word and drawn by the Holy Spirit to repent. It was an awesome time.

15

I remember as a young girl longing to be a musician and singer that would be an instrument in the hands of the Holy Spirit *to draw all men to Christ*. I often asked myself, *"Will the Lord ever call me?"*

As a teenager I would beg my father to allow me to attend youth camp in the summer, but he was very strict and wouldn't even consider allowing his daughter to spend five nights away from his supervision. Finally, my pastor intervened and said that he and his wife would be attending as counselors, and she would personally be in my cabin to supervise my every move. Church youth camp became my "heaven on earth" and it was the place that nurtured my call.

I experienced a life transformation at 16, when I received the baptism of the Holy Spirit at summer camp in Lakeland, Florida. That night I was drinking from the "well of the Holy Spirit," and became totally intoxicated. I didn't understand everything that was happening to me, but it didn't matter – I just knew that I felt closer to God than I had ever experienced and His presence was all I desired. Finally, in the wee hours of the morning, the counselors were told they would have to move everyone to their cabins. Literally, I could not move, so I was carried like a rag doll and placed on top of my bunk to "sleep it off."

The next morning I found it hard to speak and the sweetness of His presence lingered for days. I knew I was changed. I had tapped into a special place between my heavenly Father and me.

All through my teen years I questioned my pastor and every visiting minister about the call of God on my life. When a call for rededication would be presented I would rush to the front with expectation that God had something special for me. I had such a passion to serve the Lord. Growing up, I remember the many altar services where I prayed and yielded myself to the Holy Spirit, always mindful that something was maturing and developing. I was intent on not missing what I knew God had for me.

I know today's modern church has become sophisticated and streamlined, but I would not exchange that atmosphere of expectancy that was upon me in those days for anything. It was in these times that a hunger for the anointing and presence of God was developed. I remember hearing sermons that would enlighten and challenge me on the biblical definition of what a "call" was and that it was *unchangeable and irreversible.* (Romans 11:29)

During those growing up years I spent hours developing my musical talent and dreaming of the day that I would venture forth into the destiny I knew God had for me.

In 1959 I graduated from high school and it seemed the natural course of events for me to enroll at Bible College. However, during that summer I met an evangelist and within a few short months we were married. Without missing a beat, I went from high school to becoming a new bride, and right into full time evangelistic ministry. Life took on a totally different style and focus – I was a new bride with a new life and I knew I was fulfilling my call. We quickly developed into an evangelistic team, traveling from church to church singing and preaching.

In the denomination we were part of, there was no financial supportive base so we learned to trust God for everything we needed. There were no contracts, no guarantees and certainly no nice hotel rooms and gift baskets. Those were the days of the love offerings, and housing for the evangelist consisted of a back bedroom in the pastor's home or maybe a vacant Sunday school room. You simply ate wherever you were invited. Our stay could be for a weekend or, depending upon "how the Spirit moved," it could be extended for several weeks. The stories I could tell would take up another entire book but I used to say that we had *"just enough success to keep us going and plenty of failure to keep us humble."*

On December 1, 1965 we were blessed with our first daughter, Marvelyne. We continued to travel throughout the country preaching and singing and then on February 26, 1968 the Lord surprised us with twin daughters, Mary and Martha. I can remember making the statement, *"I will travel with two children but I will never travel with three."* That turned out to be the family joke because I was pregnant with two! This was a joyous time, but not an easy time.

Not only were our lives changing but also the ministry of the evangelist was rapidly changing. Where extended revival meetings had been the format for churches, it was quickly becoming an era of just weekend services. With this drastic change on the horizon we had to improvise if we were to stay true to our calling as evangelists. We had no doubt that God had called us, so we purchased a 30-foot trailer and "hit the road" with a three year old and twin baby girls. We traveled from the east coast to the west coast and all points in-between. This was an incredible time for our family and we truly experienced miraculous provision.

In 1970 we received an invitation to become the pastors of *First Assembly of God* in Montgomery, Alabama. After a great deal of prayer, we accepted. The church began to grow and experience a mighty revival and within a short time God enabled us to relocate the church to a beautiful, large facility and a new vision was birthed. Around this same time the Lord also began to bless our music and give us songs, such as *Touching Jesus Is All That Matters, Love Grew Where the Blood Fell,* and several others.

I thought for sure that we had put down deep roots; however, the restless spirit of the road was calling and against my wishes, we resigned. We quickly made plans and moved to Nashville, Tennessee to resume traveling and ministering in revival meetings. We rented a house that served as our home base. We improvised every way possible to 'stay on the road.' We had travel trailers, motor homes, and several times we rented a home in a large urban community and ministered in churches throughout that area. The girls began to express a real desire to sing and we were thrilled to include them in the ministry. They rapidly began to develop their own musical talents and ministry call. All three girls took on some form of ministry responsibility as well as singing every night during our revivals. Our oldest daughter, Marvelyne, became our product administrator at only 12 years old. Mary and Martha at 10 years of age were selecting and arranging music for the family to sing. The highlight of our ministry was working together as a family.

Christian television was fast becoming a phenomenon and we began to appear regularly on PTL Television, The 700 Club and other Christian networks throughout the country. During this time, the *song Learning to Lean* was written and won the 1977 Dove Award. We were blessed to have several recordings and also to have other people recording our songs.

Even though we experienced what most would call a successful life and ministry, there always seemed to be a strong underlying spirit of discontent. This began to be reflected in our marriage and our ministry. In 1980 the decision was made to move to Orlando, Florida and start a church in one of the fastest growing areas of the city. I prayed this would finally bring fulfillment and contentment. This was quite a transition but we all became very excited at the potential of this new ministry, and so we hit the ground running. However, it wasn't long before I observed that the same "spirit of discontent" was back. Nothing was enough, nothing appeased. As hard as I tried, I could not fix it. I began to see that even though we had shared many years together, we had very different expectations of what life was to be.

In the early years of our church, our daughters served as greeters, singers, ushers and children's workers. They took on the role of pastoring just like we did, and were a great blessing to our church. As teenagers they began developing their own musical talents and ministry. It wasn't long before they formed a contemporary Christian group called *Testament* and began to write songs and sing at many youth conferences and special events. By now our daughters were making plans to follow the call of God in their own lives.

As a family we had been through many changes and now, with the girls coming into adulthood and pursuing their futures, I looked forward to our next new season. However, nothing prepared me for what was to come.

After 28 years of marriage, my husband unexpectedly announced that there would be no more marriage or ministry. My world shattered. The life we had shared was over and the church we had worked so hard to birth would now be turned over to someone else. The intertwining of like visions and dreams was now being ripped apart and irreversibly broken. I couldn't believe what was happening.

Our lives became a nightmare of confusion, disarray and dysfunction. Plans went out the window and dreams died. My future looked very bleak. I was told, *No more discussion, this is going to happen. Nothing you can do or say will change anything. The ministry will simply be recycled with a new name and a new face!*

Finally, after several months of irreconcilable discussions, I opened the envelope and read the inevitable. **Divorce Granted.** The finality was excruciating to me.

Not only was my marriage over, but so was everything I had believed and invested in. I began to ask many questions of the Lord: Had I missed God? What went wrong? What about my call? Was I still "called" or did divorce disqualify me from ministry?

Stunned and shocked, I was forced to examine my faith, my relationship to God, and the church. No words can describe the feelings of loss and rejection.

Not sure where to turn, I began seeking answers to this puzzle. Ephesians 2:4-6 says it best: *"But God, who is rich in mercy, because of His great love with which He loved us, even when we were dead in trespasses, made us alive together with Christ (by grace you have been saved), and raised us up together, and made us sit together in the heavenly places in Christ Jesus."*

Because of *But God,* this devastation was not to be the end. As mysterious as it may sound because of *But God,,* it really was to become my beginning. *My latter was getting ready to be better than my past.* I just didn't know it yet. Little did I know *But God,* who is so rich and loves me so much is getting ready, even when I don't deserve it, to make me alive and raise me up!

There is no doubt satan thought he had delivered a fatal blow. But the same grace that I had experienced as a young girl, had followed me through every season of my life, and in my darkest hour, was there. Not only to get me through, but *to do exceedingly abundantly above all that we ask or think, according to the power that works in us!* (Ephesians 3:20) The Living Bible says: *He is able to accomplish infinitely more than we would ever dare to ask or hope.*

> **Grace says: There are no limits, no boundaries. There is increase all around – step forth!**

Grace cries out:

God is not finished with you!
There is so much more for you!
It's not too late!
You are not too old!
You are not washed-up!

I believe that at any phase of our life, even after the most heartbreaking failures, God's plan is to redeem and restore our *journey of grace.*

Grace says: There are no limits, no boundaries. There is increase all around – step forth!

NO LIMITS

You've been pressing, pushing just to get through
You've been praying, believing for something new
Your time is now – for breakthrough!
I can see, the words that He has spoken,

I can hear the sound of heavens open
The time has come for you to just receive
If you will just believe.
No limits, out the box – The ceiling tear it off
No limits we're breaking out – WALLS COME DOWN!
It's my time to dream, the impossible
I CAN DO ANYTHING
There's no limits at all,
No limits, No limits, No limits –
There's no limits now. No limits!

by Karen Greenley, Gerald Saunders, Derick Thomas
From Martha Munizzi's – NO LIMITS project:

THIS IS THE GOSPEL OF GRACE.

CHAPTER 2

Understanding Grace

> "If we are unaware of the true meaning
> of grace, there is no way that we will be
> able to comprehend the magnitude
> or awesomeness of grace."
> – Martin Luther

*U*nderstanding grace is the key to freedom in your life. Understanding grace is the power to unlock your future – your God ordained destiny. Understanding grace will open the door of blessing over your life and your family. The importance of this truth cannot be overstated!

But the doctrine of the Gospel of Grace has probably been more misunderstood, resulted in more controversy, and been used more harmfully than any other Biblical truth. If you look at history, from the early church to the present day, the pages are replete with disputes over man's interpretation of the Gospel of Grace. These theories have separated everything from families to nations. Wars have been fought and hundreds of denominations, churches, and even cults have been spawned. The truth is, grace has always been on trial. It is also true that, for you to have the abundant life God provided, you have to understand grace.

I found this axiom that I believe will give us a better understanding of grace.

God's Richest At Christ's Expense!

For many years I have heard many silly phrases and clichés that only serve to rob us of the truth of God's Word. One is, *"Grace is the ability to fulfill the lust of the flesh and not be punished for it."* Obviously that is inconsistent with the word of God. Another is the phrase: *cheap grace.* How can grace be cheap when it cost Jesus everything! As a result of so much misunderstanding, many people are rebuked rather than discipled, discouraged rather than encouraged, and many became disillusioned and never return to church. Paul declared that he labored more, not less – because of grace, (1 Corinthians 15:10). In other words, **grace brought out the very best in him**. The true biblical interpretation of grace inspires me to define my life by the principles and standards of God's Word – holy and consecrated before Him.

The Beginning of Grace

In our journey to understand grace we need to start at the beginning – Genesis 1:1. This is where grace is revealed and God's perfect plan and purpose is implemented for the foundation of life, health and happiness for all of His creation. *That's grace!*

He then shapes human beings "in His own image" and gives them dominion over His creation. God's *plan* was for Adam to reach his full potential in a perfect environment with a helpmate to share it and His *purpose* was to bring His creation into perfect union and fellowship with Him. However, sin entered the garden and dire consequences began to take effect, and for the first time the relationship that Adam and Eve had enjoyed and relied upon seems permanently severed. Crushed by guilt and shame, they now stand naked spiritually, emotionally and physically before their Creator.

Following their eviction from the garden, in Genesis 3:20, Adam refers to Eve as "the mother of all the living." In chapter 4 we see that she gives birth to Cain and exclaims with joy and praise, "With the help of the Lord I have brought forth a man!" I am sure at this point Eve probably had flashbacks of the terrible day when God came looking for her – and the awful pursuit that ensued. Now, through the precious gift of childbirth, she experiences what she thought was forever gone - something is happening! I can almost hear Eve exclaiming, "God has not forgotten me." Sometime later Eve gives birth to another son, named Abel.

After years of separation from God, Genesis 4:3 records that "*In the process of time*" an offering, prescribed by God, was to be brought by Cain and Abel. I believe that we can conclude that this is the first act of worship in human history. Through this act of obedience, reconciliation begins to take place and grace is there to witness. This is a very critical opportunity

27

in time! Strict obedience is called for. Even during the worst disobedience, rebellion and rebuke, we see God's *plan and purpose reclaimed and reinstituted.*

However, the Bible says that God rejected Cain's offering because of his presumption and disobedience but accepted Abel's because he offered a holy offering that led him into worship. In a fit of jealousy and envy, Cain murdered his own brother, Abel. This is devastating! God has one family and one of them is a murderer. This is not supposed to happen.

In Genesis 4:25-26 we read that Adam knew his wife again, and she bore a son and named him Seth, *"For God has appointed another seed for me instead of Abel, whom Cain killed."* There it is! Grace in action! God recognized Seth as the foundation stone, and Bible scholars have written that he was "set" or "appointed" to take up the work and mission of Abel. Seth also had a son, named Enosh, and the Bible records that after the generation of Enosh, *"men began to call on the name of the Lord!"*

Enosh's grandparents, Adam and Eve, were God's all-time disappointments. But we must remind ourselves continually that God never gives up because we are His primary *purpose.* His grace screams out, *"No, let me redeem, let me display who I am."*

Continuing on through ten generations since Adam, we read in Genesis Chapter 6, disturbing reports that with each generation man is descending into greater wickedness *following every evil their mind could conceive.* In fact, the Bible says that *God was so grieved at what He saw and heard that He repented that He ever made man.* Viewing the wickedness and perversion, God made the decision to set in motion a plan to judge the earth and save them from themselves.

All through the generations we have seen a pervasive characteristic displayed by God that gave hope to the hopeless and spoke faith to the faithless. That pervasive characteristic that keeps popping up at every disappointing turn is now, for the first time, given expression and it has found a name in Genesis 6:8, *"But Noah found grace in the eyes of the LORD."* Yes, for the first time it has a name and the name is: **GRACE!**

The life of Noah is a perfect picture to understanding grace. When the whole world was full of wickedness and chaos, God's focus was on judgment; but there was a righteous man named Noah. The Bible says that God looked upon him with such favor and acceptance that his focus moved from judgment to grace. God could look at one man, and change His mind. This is a testimony of hope for every person to move past the grief, the heartache, the disappointments and rejections into God's provision of grace.

God established nine covenants with Noah, from Genesis 6:18 through Genesis 9:17. I love the verse in Genesis 9:13, *"I set My rainbow in the cloud, and it shall be for the sign of the covenant between Me and the earth."* What is this manifestation in the sky? It is God's pouring out His favor and blessing to an undeserving earth.

Beginning in Genesis 12:2 we read how God established His covenant of favor and blessing upon Abraham that continued throughout the lives of his children and the nation of Israel *"I will make you a great nation; I will bless you and make your name great; and you shall be a blessing."* (Genesis 12:2)

God's covenants are not challenged or changed as a result of our circumstances. It is satan's delight to manipulate our emotions and make us feel that, due to our failure, God no longer remembers us; however, the Bible is very clear when it says, *"God is ever mindful of his covenant."* (Psalm 111:5) With that in mind – we should always, with an attitude of praise and a lifestyle of victory, remember we are *"covenant people,"* and as covenant people we all have a beginning journey of grace. Romans 4:16 says that we are now part of that covenant: *"Therefore it is of faith that it might be according to grace, so that the promise might be sure to all the seed, not only to those who are of the law, but also to those who are of the faith of Abraham, who is the father of us all."* We are blessed right alongside Abraham!

When Jesus came to this earth as a baby, the Bible says that grace was activated in His life: *"And the Child grew and became strong in spirit, filled with wisdom; and the grace of God was upon Him."* (Luke 2:40) Grace, the divine favor and blessing of God, rested upon Jesus Christ throughout His life, death, resurrection and ascension. Jesus is grace personified!

Luke 2:52 also records that Jesus increased in wisdom and stature and in favor with God and men. This is astounding that even Christ himself grew in the favor of God! Yes, He was human by choice, but He increased in the graces of the Holy Spirit. John 1:14 says, "And the Word became flesh and dwelt among us, and we beheld His glory, the glory as of the only begotten of the Father, *full of grace and truth.*" Jesus completely embodies grace and truth and as a result men of every race, tribe or color can be brought to salvation.

Grace Is God's Unmerited Favor

Our beginning point is to ask a very important question: WHAT IS GRACE? Grace has been expressed as *"God's unmerited favor."*

Though I had been a part of the church all of my life the true revelation of the *Gospel of Grace* had never been made real to me. In fact, for many years my understanding or should

> *Grace has nothing to do with human effort but has everything to do with a loving Heavenly Father.*

I say, lack of understanding, was formed and filtered through a set of opinions, hidden agendas and conditions set by the denomination and the local church. I was taught that if you did what was right, went to church and obeyed the rules, divorce and other bad things would not happen. It wasn't until I went to Bible School and began to study such subjects as, *Understanding Righteousness, Blood Covenant* and *Creation Realities*, did real understanding come.

31

It may sound extremely simple but I came to the realization, through the Word of God, that grace is free! I can just hear the response, "Of course, I know that!" But in so much of our traditional thinking, we believe that grace is linked in some shape or form to human performance or human merit. The good news is that *grace has nothing to do with human effort but has everything to do with a loving Heavenly Father.* Ephesians 1:7 says *"In Him we have redemption through His blood, the forgiveness of sins, according to the riches of His grace."* It has nothing to do with you and everything to do with Him!

When I was 16 years old I stood around an open fire at a church youth camp and committed my life to the service of the Lord. It seemed easy to believe God had great things for me and would direct my life as I followed Him. Twenty-eight years later, after devastation and what seemed like failure, it wasn't so easy to believe. At that point of my life if you had said, *"Faith, God has great things for you, just believe,"* I couldn't have processed it. I had no idea of the profound gift of grace that was available to me. I lacked the necessary understanding of the process to access the abundance of grace available.

Now here I stand, years later, teaching about grace. I still startle myself when I make this statement, *"Human merit rules out grace."* You see, you add human effort or merit to the equation and it ceases to be grace. Dr. Robert McGee, in his life-changing book *Search for Significance,* would call it "human performance." God says performance is not necessary because *"by grace are ye saved through faith, it is a gift."* In fact the Living

Bible really opens up the understanding of Ephesians 1:7-8 when it says, *"God is so rich in **kindness** that he purchased our freedom through the blood of his Son, and our sins are forgiven. He has showered his kindness on us, along with all wisdom and understanding."*

There is nothing for you to do but receive it. Are you afraid of presumption? How can you be presumptuous when God states emphatically that He will shower His kindness on you as well as all wisdom and understanding?

Are you caught in the trap of *human performance?* Romans 2:4 says, *"It is God's kindness that leads us to repentance."* Not a set of rigid man-made rules and regulations that we have to adhere to. This verse is in direct contrast to the hell-fire and brimstone sermons I heard as a child. Many years ago I heard a preacher say, *"It's okay to preach about hell – just don't sound like you are glad people are going there!"*

Through my childhood God was presented to me like a big ogre with a list of do's and don'ts, ready to pounce on everyone. A lot of emphasis was placed on outward

> *Grace establishes us and enables us to serve God.* 彩

appearance, especially for the women. I remember when I was a young girl makeup was considered a definite 'no.' I longed to enhance my appearance with a little color but I was made to feel that if I did, my salvation was in jeopardy. In fact, there wasn't much we could do that didn't jeopardize our salvation.

For years I lived with a cloud thinking that I had to 'prove myself' in some way to God. The sad thing is that everyone around me felt the same way. We sang about being free but we were not free! We were bound with our own legalism. Satan's main agenda is to shackle us with feelings of unworthiness and shame, in order to render us helpless and hopeless. I have said many times to our Bible School students, *"The devil doesn't care what ditch you get into just as long as you get off the road."* It can even be a religious ditch.

> *Grace gives joy,*
> *when joy is gone.*
> *Grace gives hope,*
> *when hope is gone.*
> *Grace makes a way*
> *where there is no way.*

Grace Is God's Power in Operation

Grace is ever working, developing, anointing and abounding in and through you. It's through His grace that we can rise to the level to be and to do all that God has called us to be and to do. (Romans 5:1, 2)

Sadly, for many, grace is viewed as a passive attitude that God has! It is not passive but is ACTIVE! It is divine enablement to bring us to a new level of the manifestation of the power of God.

Grace is the means whereby we find salvation. Grace establishes us and enables us to serve God. Grace meets our every need. Grace is active and working in our lives.

Proof of this is when the Apostle Paul said, *"According to the grace of God which was given to me, as a wise master builder."* (1 Corinthians 3:10) As a teacher and mentor, he states over and over that abundant grace, full provision and divine enablement, were given to Him to accomplish what God had called him to do.

In Hebrews 4:16 we are told *"Come boldly to the throne of grace, that we may obtain mercy and find grace to help in time of need."* This is not passive, this is active! We are given an invitation to walk boldly to the throne of God and make a withdrawal of mercy and grace. WHEN? When we need it. Hallelujah! This is exciting! An invitation to not just come, but come boldly and confidently to God's throne, His throne called "grace."

Grace Is a Waymaker

> Grace gives joy, when joy is gone.
> Grace gives hope, when hope is gone.
> Grace makes a way where there is no way.

One of the most outstanding pictures of grace in the entire Bible is found in the book of Acts, with the story of a deacon. The church is on the rise and Acts Chapter 6 reports that the Gospel is spreading like wildfire. There is one man who takes center stage, speaking with such authority and power that *"they were not able to resist the wisdom and the Spirit by which he spoke so he became marked for annihilation."* (Acts 6:10)

As this man preached, the look in the eyes of the crowd became a warning – they were not happy with his message. With every word he spoke he knew he was nearer to danger. But he did not turn. He did not run. As he continued to speak the Word of the Lord, their anger became so vile and so intense that a mob mentality took over. Acts 7:55 says *"But he, being full of the Holy Spirit, gazed into heaven and saw the glory of God, and Jesus standing at the right hand of God, and said, 'Look! I see the heavens opened and the Son of Man standing at the right hand of God!' Then they cried out with a loud voice, stopped their ears, and ran at him with one accord; and they cast him out of the city and stoned him. And the witnesses laid down their clothes at the feet of a young man named Saul. And they stoned Stephen as he was calling on God and saying,*

There is nothing that needs to be done to merit God's grace.

'Lord Jesus, receive my spirit.' Then he knelt down and cried out with a loud voice, 'Lord, do not charge them with this sin.' And when he had said this, he fell asleep."

Hearing such a horrible story many people, even believers, are consumed with gloom and despair, saying, *"What a shame. He was so young. He had so much potential. How could it have happened?"* My friend, Stephen was a man with a message, and grace enabled him to deliver that message. As Mr. Paul Harvey says, *"Now here's the rest of the story."* Acts 7:58 says that a young man was standing in the front row, observing, and the witnesses laid down their clothes at the feet of a young man named Saul who later became the Apostle Paul.

Grace Will Sustain

Grace will sustain us through every situation and even during our infancy stage of spiritual growth. It is so important that we teach new Christians and those who struggle with a myriad of issues, that grace sustains even in the times of temptation, weakness and challenges. The theme should be: Persevere and let grace bear you up.

Throw away all those old notions, preconceived ideas, traditions of men, and false interpretations of the gospel of grace and embrace the unlimited, unadulterated, heavenly, unexplainable, grace of God. Friends, if you feel inadequate, remember God does not disqualify people. He provides the grace, through Jesus Christ, to make you more than qualified.

In my journey I found grace is a principle Bible doctrine that, with the revelation of the Holy Spirit, will activate a dynamic faith-filled life.

The Bible makes it clear that:

- *There is nothing we can do to merit God's grace.*
- *There is nothing that needs to be done to merit God's grace.*
- *There is nothing we can refrain from doing to merit God's grace.*
- *Grace cannot be earned.*
- *Grace is that place where there are no limits, no boundaries.*
- *Grace is truly liberating.*

I want to give you the words of an awesome song that I believe encapsulates everything that I have been trying to say. My daughter, Mary Alessi and our dear friend, Cindy Cruse-Ratcliff wrote this song at my piano, entitled, *I Am Always Welcome*.

I Am Always Welcome

Your presence a refuge for me where I am always welcome
Your arms are a resting place where I can always go
Your Spirit is calling me and I can answer willingly
The door to You is open wide and I am always welcome

Your truth and life I find inside
And I am always welcome
The peace inside I can't describe
And I am always welcome
You draw me in to where you dwell
And I'm welcome
Where you are is where I want to be
In your presence

So draw me to your side wide, pour your love on me
Where you are is where I long to be – in your presence
Where you are – Where you dwell
I am always welcome
You draw me in to where You dwell
And I'm welcome

CHAPTER 3

Grace Is Amazing!

*T*o say he was a man full of evil would be a fair description. A man so controlled by his own anger, hate and prejudice that he hunted down, tortured, and even killed kind, loving people who had never caused harm. Convinced of his own superiority, he sought political covering to carry out his cruelty. He actively attempted to organize a system where the innocent could be murdered with celebration. He pursued permission to bring about the deaths of people who believed differently from what he thought was best. He had his own version of "godliness."

Believing he was justified, he personally spent time and energy searching out and uncovering the hiding places of these righteous people. It was during one of these expeditions that he had a head-on collision with Grace.

The infamous Saul of Tarsus, now better known as the Apostle Paul, recounts this dramatic encounter in Acts 26, as his conversion to Christ. He openly confesses to the life he lived; a life full of hate, spent hunting down and killing men and women who had accepted Jesus as the Messiah. But on this fateful day his mission was interrupted, when suddenly he was surrounded by a great light and a voice from heaven saying, *"Saul? Why are you persecuting me?"*

Bewildered, he asked the voice, *"Who are you, Lord?"*

The voice spoke back, *"I am Jesus, whom you are persecuting. But rise and stand on your feet – because I have appeared to you for this purpose: to make you a minister and a witness – so that all people may receive forgiveness of sin and be sanctified by faith."*

At that point Saul is given clear instructions as to the purpose of his call. The Lord spoke and said that he is to become a minister, both to the Jews and Gentiles. He is to be a profound witness to what he has seen and will walk in a revelation of things to come.

> *'Justification' is the act of God whereby our legal standing in heaven is changed and we are declared righteous.*

Wow! Saul was, by his own admission, the chief of sinners. The baddest of the bad. The worst of the worse. Now, here he is raised up as a chosen vessel to carry the Gospel of Jesus Christ to the world.

I do not believe it is a coincidence that God picked this particular sinner and introduced him so dramatically to the awesomeness of Grace. In one moment, his life was forever altered, and this murderer called Saul became the great Apostle Paul, minister of the Gospel. It was not his education that qualified him – *it was grace.* It was not his merit that empowered him – *it was grace.* It was not his ability that anointed him – *it was grace.*

It was Grace, the unmerited favor
and blessing of Almighty God.

I believe that it is extremely important that we explore the question, why is Grace so amazing? Grace is amazing because of what it provides!

Grace Is Amazing Because It Provides Justification

Justification is the act of God whereby our legal standing in heaven is changed and we are declared righteous. It is by justification that we can lay claim to all the good things of God.

Romans 3:24, in the Amplified Version says, *"All are justified and made upright and in right standing with God, freely and gratuitously by His grace [His unmerited favor and mercy], through the redemption which is [provided] in Christ Jesus."* Isn't that amazing?

Plainly said: We are *"justified"* (just as if we never sinned) and made in right standing with God – without cost – simply because God is good and Jesus provided for it through His life, death and resurrection.

If you were to ask the local congregation, *"Would everyone here that is righteous please raise your hand?"*

> *The cross of Jesus is a public demonstration of God's righteousness.* 𝒮𝔞

you might get a few hands but I can guarantee you the overwhelming majority of church people would respond, *"No, the Bible says that our righteousness is as filthy rags."* That is an answer but not the correct answer. Yes, my righteousness and your righteousness is worthless. However, we are not talking about our righteousness or our ability or goodness.

2 Corinthians 5:21 says, *"For He made Him who knew no sin to be sin for us, that we might become the righteousness of God in Him."* The cross of Jesus is a public demonstration of God's righteousness.

Our confession should always be *confessing our right-standing with God!* One of the ways the devil defeats us is by what comes out of our own mouths. Many times we are our worst enemy. The Bible declares four times that *"the just shall live by faith."* As *just* people we have been *declared righteous* and now we are in perfect standing with God. (Romans 3:24) Now that's a confession! By keeping scriptures like this at the forefront of our confession we now can *"with boldness and confidence approach the throne of God and ask what we will and it will be done."* (Hebrews 4:14)

Satan loves to attack our boldness and confidence with his vicious lies, but the best thing in our defense is to agree with Titus. *"For we ourselves were also once foolish, disobedient, deceived, serving various lusts and pleasures, living in malice and envy, hateful and hating one another. But when the kindness and the love of God our Savior toward man appeared, not by works of righteousness which we have done, but according to His mercy He saved us, through the washing of regeneration and renewing of the Holy Spirit, whom He poured out on us abundantly through Jesus Christ our Savior, that having been justified by His grace we should become heirs according to the hope of eternal life."* (Titus 3:3,4)

This should be our focus: The amazing grace of God that has justified us, made us righteous and now we have been made heirs. That's right, you have an inheritance..

Dr. Robert McGee's book, ***Search for Significance***, says that justification puts us in the position to boldly confess: *I am deeply loved, completely forgiven, fully pleasing, totally accepted, and complete in Christ.*

It is incomprehensible to think that even in our sinful state, God demonstrated His own love toward us, by allowing Christ to die for us plus justify us. (Romans 5:8,9) Now it's time to say, *Thank you Jesus!*

We are no longer performance based. No! Thank God we are now grace-based!

Grace Is Amazing Because It Provides Reconciliation

Reconcile means to *resolve and to settle.* I am reminded of an old song that was a favorite when I was growing up. *The old account was settled long ago. And my record's clear today for he washed my sins away and the old account was settled long ago.*

Colossians 1:20-21 says, *"And by Him to reconcile all things to Himself, by Him, whether things on earth or things in heaven, having made peace through the blood of His cross. And you, who once were alienated and enemies in your mind by wicked works, yet now He has reconciled."* So many Christians are still fighting battles they have already won and still pursuing territories they already have the title deed for. All because we are still trying to do something to prove that we are accepted. **It's all settled and it's all resolved.**

Haven't you heard? *This is unconditional acceptance.* Acceptance without pause or question. You mean I don't have to prove anything? Exactly! We are made acceptable through the cross! <u>There is no greater theme in the scripture than the reconciliation of man to God.</u> Thank God! God's gift of grace has given us total "reconciliation." We are completely acceptable to God. You see, it's a 'done deal.' It's not something you decide – it's decided for you – YOU ARE ACCEPTED! Now step into the grace that is yours.

Grace Is Amazing Because It Provides Propitiation

Propitiate is an old English word which means "to appease." The blood of Christ was a sufficient propitiation (or appeasement) for the sins of the whole world. (1 John 2:2)

I love to make this pronouncement, "God is not mad at you! Nothing you can do will incur God's wrath! This scripture makes it clear that His arms are open wide and through the *gift of grace* God's wrath has been completely satisfied."

For so many years of my life I thought that most of the time God was about half mad at me. I learned that is simply not true. The truth is, God is viewing you and me through the blood sacrifice of His dear Son. *His wrath has been fully satisfied!* Recognize that the devil will do everything he can to *kill, steal and destroy* God's plan for your life because this is *his mission.* (John 10:10) However *Jesus came to give us abundant life, to repossess what was stolen and restore what the locust has consumed!* (Joel 2:25) This is all accomplished by grace.

> **What some may regard as a disqualifying situation, God declares, "This is your place of grace!"** 🙈

Grace Is Amazing Because It Provides Regeneration

Ephesians 2:5-7 says, *"even when we were dead in trespasses, (we are) made alive together with Christ (by grace you have been saved), and raised us up together, and made us sit together in the heavenly places in Christ Jesus."*

Titus 3:5 tells us that *"according to His mercy He saved us, through the washing of regeneration and renewing of the Holy Spirit."*

My past is not a "black spot." It is not a hindrance, handicap, nor a stigma or blight. My past is *forgiven*, washed away, under the blood of Jesus, and

He calls me *righteous*. The message of the gospel of grace is *forgiveness and restoration*. Don't allow any one, Christian or non-Christian, to try to disqualify you based on past failures. Forgiveness isn't something we work toward – it's something we embrace – every moment of every day.

Some of the most effective ministries are birthed out of brokenness and failure. Prison ministries are started by former inmates. Former addicts who have known the affects of alcohol and drug abuse now become support for others struggling with addictions. Former prostitutes become *ministers of reconciliation*. These are people who are finding their *place of grace*.

What some may regard as a
disqualifying situation, God declares,

This is your place of grace!

What you may view as a
failure, my God says,

This is your place of grace!

What someone else may regard as
insurmountable, God says,

This is your place of grace!

Rather than a "stigma" or "blight" your past can become the drawing force for your ministry. Rather than feel handicapped, this will become *your stepping stone into greatness*. You need not feel *less than*, in fact, because of the grace of God, celebrate the fact that you are *more than*.

This unmerited favor and grace of God has blessed and transformed my life. What the devil meant for evil, God has dramatically turned into good, and it has served to propel me into God's finest and best. If I had listened to the worn out clichés and religious rhetoric that were being spoken over me, I would have given up. But, thank God, the revelation of His word was opened to me and I embraced it with everything within me. As a result I found my place of grace – the place where God's favor and blessing are manifested continually upon me and my family.

Friends, expand your thinking and concept of grace by embracing the Word of God in all its fullness. Allow the anointing of the Holy Spirit to enlarge your capacity and embrace the amazing grace that God has bestowed upon us.

❧ *Early Years* ❧

CHAPTER 4

Grace: A Blessing of Choice

One day you'll look back and thank God for every trial and test you've gone through!

God must be trying to get your attention!

If you just fast long enough, and pray hard enough, God will have to turn this around!

Don't you just love religious pat answers?

These Christian comforts are designed to satisfy the "why?" but all they really do is add to the confusion. There are times when "religious answers" are not appropriate and do not suffice. Sadly, this is religious rhetoric, repeated as a substitute for a genuine answer from the Word of God. I should know because I have given plenty of them and I have had many given to me.

In the throes of human emotion even favorite scriptures can seem hollow. During my darkest hours

I found myself asking, *is Romans 8:28 really true? Do all things work together for good to those who love God, to those who are the called according to His purpose? Will there come a time when God can use all that has happened for good? Is there actually a place of blessing? How is it possible? How can anger, separation, destruction and devastation ever bring 'good?'*

It is so easy to feel like you have all the answers when everything in your life is going well! It's easy to hand out condolences and encouragements when you are standing in the midst of a good situation and life is on track! But life doesn't always stay "on track." Sometimes it feels completely out of your control.

One day during a terribly difficult time in my life, I felt shamed and judged because of someone else's choice. Having a first rate pity party, I looked heavenward and cried out, *"Lord, it can't get any worse than this!"*

As soon as I said it I felt God's rebuke and He said very profoundly to me, *"Faith, it can get a lot worse than this."* At that moment the future became like a fast moving video. In my mind I could see images depicting not only a dark future for me but also for my three daughters. The ideals that I cherished were discarded. Everything seemed out of focus and covered in confusion, and lack. I knew that God had spoken to me and was calling me to better things, but I didn't know where to start. It seemed like a wall too high to climb, and a valley too far to walk.

I made an appointment with my pastor but even he seemed overwhelmed with my situation and strongly recommended that I see a Christian counselor. The prospect of pouring out my emotions to a professional listener was not at the top of my list of things to do. I was skeptical, and a little cynical, but I decided to go ahead and make the appointment. I arrived at the doctor's office fully prepared to make sure he understood "my side of the story" and how wronged I had been. Through tears I shared with him all of my heartbreak. When I thought that he had a full picture of my grief, I sat back for his consolation.

After patiently listening to me graphically and emotionally share my story, he leaned over his desk, and instead of words of comfort he asked me this question: "How long do you intend to carry this offense?"

I was horrified and indignant. "This is not MY OFFENSE! This was done to me. My anger is totally justified! Don't you see the facts? Weren't you listening?"

I will never forget his next words. He said, "Faith, if you do not allow forgiveness into your life I can guarantee that within three to five years you will be facing a list of physiological problems that no doctor can cure." He began to explain to me how our emotions effect us physically. He elaborated how heart disease, arthritis, digestive problems and many other diseases can stem from unforgiveness. In other words – our emotions have a profound affect on our physical bodies. I quickly began to make my defense. He said to me, "Faith, unforgiveness has no defense. Your body doesn't know the difference; you may have been wronged – you may have wronged somebody – but you still have to release the bitterness, the anger and the malice, and forgive."

When the appointment was over I went to my car with my mind whirling. I felt intense anger but at the same time, as strange as it my sound, it was mixed with hope. I knew one thing for sure. *There was no way I was going to be branded with the scars of this for the rest of my life.* As soon as I unlocked the door to my car I felt as if the heavens had opened and I was within reach of my greatest breakthrough.

> *You do not have to jump up and play "sunshine and happiness," but you do have to intentionally choose your thoughts and actions each and every day.*

I began to hear the Spirit of the Lord speaking to me, *"If you engage in bitterness and unforgiveness, anger will control your life. If you choose this way you will heap upon yourself, your children and your children's children untold heartache and sickness. It's your decision!"*

The Lord brought to my remembrance Deuteronomy 28, where Moses speaks to the Children of Israel about the opportunity for blessing and cursing. *"If you diligently obey the voice of the LORD your God, to observe carefully all His commandments which I command you today, that the LORD your God will set you high above all nations of the earth, and all these blessings shall come upon you and overtake you, because you obey the voice of the LORD your God."*

There it was. The blessing of choice. Kindness, favor and grace – upon me and my house, there for the choosing. Just like a giant sheet spread before me I saw *BLESSING and CURSING.* I saw a vision of my children and grandchildren to be. I saw sickness and health spread before me. At that moment it was in my hands. It was MY CHOICE.

Without a doubt I chose blessing! I immediately looked toward heaven and asked God to forgive me. Then I addressed satan:

"No way, satan, you have not won.
Today is the first day of the rest of my life.
I choose to forgive!
This situation will not take its toll on my
physical body or my emotions.
I am on my way to total victory.
I am healed inside and out!
I also declare that this will not affect my
children and their families.
In fact, it will become a 'stepping stone' to our destiny.
It will build character and integrity into
each one of us. I declare that God will use each
of us for His divine plan and purpose. Hallelujah!"

Once I verbalized it, I then began the task of walking it out. I wish I could report that it is a one-time decision. But it is not. Choosing the blessing – choosing to walk in forgiveness is on going. It's a choice that is made daily, sometimes moment-to-moment and often through gritted teeth – but it is made! You do not have to have a great moment of declarations to others. It is between you and God. You don't have to jump up and play "sunshine and happiness," but you have to intentionally choose your thoughts and actions each and every day. It gets easier the more often you make the right choice.

Hard times can only produce faith if we make the right choice. ᙏᙓ

There is a very compelling story from the book of Genesis that I believe can give us incredible insight concerning grace. It is the story of Joseph, a handsome young man, protected, somewhat coddled by an indulgent father. Yet his childhood became the training ground for his God ordained destiny. As a youngster he stood for righteousness and often had prophetic dreams about his family. In his naïveté he would share these dreams with his brothers. These dreams often had Joseph as the hero, and his brothers were not very excited about that prospect. Their jealousy and envy caused them to conspire and devise a plan to rid themselves of this annoyance by selling him into slavery. He was taken a long way from home and, seemingly, even farther away from the realization of his heaven-sent dreams of his destiny. However, Joseph's God was still working out His purposes and plans. For fourteen years, during which he faced rejection, scandal, and imprisonment, the favor of God never left Joseph's life.

When Joseph at last came face to face with his brothers; the same brothers who had caused all of the chaos and pain in his life, Genesis tells us, Joseph looked them in the eye, and confidently and gently proclaimed, *"But as for you, you meant evil against me; but God meant it for good."*

How could he make such a statement? Where was the anger? This was Joseph's opportunity to set the record straight; his chance to apprise them of the horror and abuse he had endured! But nowhere do we read about Joseph indicting his brothers, or God, for his circumstances. Through disappointment after disappointment, Joseph stood faithful and continually chose the Blessing. As a result God used him mightily.

Not only does Romans 8:28 say that *"all things work together for good,"* but we must finish the verse, *"to those that love God."* No, it won't be the same for everybody. There is a clear distinction – those who love God and those who do not love God. In Deuteronomy 28 Moses writes that God makes the distinction between the *obedient* and the *disobedient*.

Yes, the choice is ours – blessing or cursing. Let me pose this question: How can afflictions become blessings?

> *When you choose the blessing rather than the cursing, God's Spirit joins our spirit and together is working FOR OUR GOOD.* 🙏

Hard times can only produce faith if we make the right choice. For the ones who choose the blessing – the worst of circumstances can bring forgiveness, peace, and love but the wrong choice can produce rebellion, anger, impatience, and even hatred.

The magnitude of the blessing we will receive is based upon the faith and trust in which we choose to walk, and thereby access a level of grace we never thought possible.

The Psalmist David sang:

*You have turned for me my
mourning into dancing;*

*You have put off my sackcloth and
clothed me with gladness,*

*To the end that my glory may sing praise
to You and not be silent.*

*O LORD my God, I will give
thanks to You forever.*

Ps 30:11-12

When you choose the blessing rather than the cursing, God's Spirit joins our spirit and together is working FOR OUR GOOD. However, if our spirit is full of unforgiveness and anger there is nothing for God to work with. As we submit in obedience to His perfect will, His grace will cause the worst of circumstances to contribute to our worth. It is only then that we can say *all things work together for good.*

It's not magic produced on God's part – it's the principles of the blessing in action because we have made the right choice. We have chosen to turn the curse into a blessing.

Hebrews 12:11

*"Now no chastening seems to be
joyful for the present, but painful;
Nevertheless, afterward it yields the
peaceable fruit of righteousness to those
who have been trained by it."*

My friend, this is very key in dealing with any circumstance in your life. In many cases an offense seems legitimate. You have been done wrong! Your anger may seem justified and you can sing like the country singer, *"Somebody done me wrong song."* Bitterness, anger and resentment will take a toll in your body and in your emotions, as well as affecting all of your relationships – including the most important one: the one with your Heavenly Father.

The more you refuse to be angry and bitter, the more you will experience the blessing, the kindness, the favor and grace of Almighty God – upon you and your house. No, it won't be easy and it will not happen all at one time. It is a process. There will be many opportunities to indulge yourself and have a pity party. But the result of experiencing the blessing of grace is simply too awesome. Why do bad things happen to Godly people? I don't know. Sometimes it simply doesn't make sense.

But this I do know: God will take every situation and use it as an opportunity to bring the manifestation of His grace into your life and produce a blessing you cannot contain. **The CHOICE is yours.**

CHAPTER 5

Grace to Endure

I never thought the word D-I-V-O-R-C-E would be a part of my life, but here I was holding divorce papers in my hand! It was excruciating! It was as if I were struck deaf, dumb and blind all at the same time – almost physically and definitely spiritually. I didn't believe what my ears were hearing and what my eyes were seeing. I felt like I was entering a dark, scary tunnel.

The words reverberated. Divorce. I thought that nothing this bad could possibly happen to our family. Not because we were special, but because I thought we had obeyed all the rules. We believed the Bible; we prayed together, we attended church. We did all the "right" things. A lifetime of being in the church and almost 30 years of full time ministry did not prepare me for this. How could this have happened?

As a young adult life was good, almost perfect! I thought I was married to the love of my life and we became partners in marriage and ministry. For almost three decades we traveled throughout the United States singing our songs and preaching the gospel. Our lives always revolved around the church. We appeared on many international television programs and had a very exciting and fulfilling ministry – so I thought.

One of the very first songs I learned to sing and play on the piano was, *Jesus loves me this I know for the Bible tells me so* but now I didn't feel that love – the song was gone! I rationalized, "If Jesus loves me so much how He could have let this happen to me?" That seemed an appropriate question. I believed that if you lived the right way that nothing this bad or painful could happen to you. And surely if you prayed hard enough and long enough God had to make the situation change!

However, the man that I knew to be my husband, lover, father of my children, mentor and pastor said that he did not want this life anymore – the life that we had shared as a couple and as a family. He wanted to move on!

It was paralyzing! I had no idea how to move on. Every point of reference for me revolved around our lives together. From the moment I first realized my husband was leaving, I became reactive. Not proactive. It was as if I became spastic, going in all directions. I began to do almost everything anyone suggested; I prayed, fasted, bound, rebuked, even screamed, but there was no relief. I tried quoting my favorite Bible verses. Then I switched to all the religious clichés I knew – nothing worked!

My faith was truly put to the test and every resource that I knew failed me. As far as I knew the devil had entered my home and delivered a fatal blow. How could you change the facts? It was a done deal! It was over. Almost 30 years of marriage, family, ministry and reputation wiped away with the stroke of a pen. No financial settlement, no income – just debt that, in my ignorance, was assigned to me.

The most cherished thing in my life – my family – was torn to pieces. The deep commitment that I thought held us together and had always sustained us was discarded like a worn out shoe. It was as if it had no importance and no value. The ministry that we had built together and shared as a couple and a family was simply to be recycled with new names and new faces. Everything within me tried to adjust, to make whatever changes were necessary because I did not desire divorce. Every attempt to reconcile was like getting bitten by a venomous snake. Friends and relatives held to various opinions – most not really knowing what to do.

Some would point out to me the scriptural grounds for divorce as they counseled me to see an attorney, while others held firmly that *if you pray and fast enough, God is required to turn it around.* This confusion and indecision became unbearable. The fall out with family and friends, as well as with the church, was enormous in its circumference.

In church we casually throw around the phrase *"The Lord told me to tell you…"* without realizing the weight, and often the pain, those words can carry. I will never forget the day that a well meaning Christian friend of mine called to tell me that the Lord had spoken to her. I was always eager to embrace any bit of Godly wisdom available. Her words, however, broke my heart.

She said, "I've been praying and the Lord told me to tell you that if you will fast and pray for thirty days, God will supernaturally restore your home." That sounded good, right? However, what she did not know was that very day I had received a shocking phone call informing me that my former husband had already remarried, just three days after the divorce was finalized. Without knowing it, my friend had imposed upon me a tremendous burden of guilt. Had I not prayed and fasted enough?

I had always regarded Sunday morning as the highlight of my week and approached it with anticipation, however, now Sunday morning church had become agonizing. Sometimes I told myself that it was just easier to stay home, but I forced myself to do what I knew was right. One particular Sunday it seemed especially difficult to put one foot in front of the other and proceed to the church. I walked into the sanctuary just in time for a lady minister that I knew to spot me. As she approached, I cringed. Everything within me dreaded that moment. *What was she going to say? How do I respond? How much does she know? I'm embarrassed – ashamed.*

I thought to myself, *If I speak first then I can steer the conversation.* So I blurted out, "Shirley, how are you?" She quickly smiled a great big smile of anticipation and eagerly began to speak to me.

"Faith you're not going to believe it, but God has given me a profound word for you."

I felt an icy fear grip my heart. I knew that she was aware that my marriage was in trouble but there were many circumstances of which she had no knowledge. Cringing, I thought to myself, *Oh, no, here it comes.* I braced for the worst.

As she began to speak my defenses broke. The fear and shame I felt melted away as the anointing filled that space, and I began to cry. She said, "God has spoken to me to tell you not to carry the burden of prayer for your marriage and family but I am to pray for you."

Now, here is a person not really understanding all the implications, saying, *don't pray because God has said that I am to pray for you.* This made no sense to me; however her words brought revelation and piercing truth into my soul and my spirit.

What she did not know, and as peculiar as it may sound, was that prayer had become a real source of confusion and despair for me. I was so filled with worry and anxiety that when I tried to enunciate my need, the reality of my situation would overwhelm me and confusion would set in. My emotions would then take over. At that point I knew I was not praying effectively but I didn't know what to do about it. I thought that effective prayer had to be emotional, with great physical effort and intensity. I was convinced the louder I prayed, the more God listened and this would produce a more effective prayer. And, of course, it didn't hurt to scream at satan a little bit.

> *Praise is an integral part of our deliverance and it must be about Him and focused on who He is.* 🙏

I then asked her this question, "What did God show you that I need to be doing?" Without hesitation she looked directly into my eyes and spoke with authority, "Faith, the Lord said that He wants you to praise – nothing more, nothing less." This was incomprehensible to me! I could not believe it! I couldn't wrap my brain around this whole encounter, but spiritually, I knew it was God saying, *Faith, I've got your back.* During the wee hours of the morning my dear friend, Shirley Cook, diligently began to pray for me. This was a profound witness that God in His grace and mercy would speak to someone to "stand in the gap" for my family and me. As I cried out to the Lord, He brought to my remembrance a scripture passage in Book of Psalms where David faced his own feelings of despair.

> *I waited patiently for the LORD; And He inclined to me, And heard my cry. He also brought me up out of a horrible pit, Out of the miry clay, And set my feet upon a rock, And established my steps. He has put a new song in my mouth – Praise to our God; Many will see it and fear, And will trust in the LORD. (Ps 40:1-3)*

As I began to pour over these verses the anointing of the Holy Sprit brought revelation to me and began to show me this passage as a step-by-step formula to get out of despair.

Psalms 40:1-3 from the Psalmist David:

♦ *I waited patiently for the LORD,*

David gives us the perfect answer in this verse on how to respond when the anticipated answer does not come. This is the assignment: You wait and you wait with patience. At the same time you continue with earnest, persevering prayer. *"Rest in the LORD, and wait patiently for Him; Do not fret because of him who prospers in his way."* (Psalm 37:7)

♦ *And He inclined to me,*

The indication here is that God was receptive and favor was present - Grace is on the scene. Remember: *"God is our refuge and strength, a very present help in trouble."* (Psalm 46:1)

♦ *And He heard my cry...*

David acknowledges that God heard his cry. Know that God does hear and He does answer prayer. *"Be anxious for nothing, but in everything by prayer and supplication, with thanksgiving, let your requests be made known to God; and the peace of God, which surpasses all understanding, will guard your hearts and minds through Christ Jesus."* (Philippians 4:6-7)

- ◆ *He also brought me up out of a horrible pit...*
  In this reference the word "pit" means a prison
  or dungeon. Several Bible commentaries de-
  scribed this pit "as a dark tunnel full of noise."
  In Psalms 18:16 David says, *"God reached down
  from on high and took hold of me."* Throughout
  the Psalms, God is referred to as a *'rescuer, lifter,
  restorer and protector.'*

- ◆ *And set my feet upon a rock, and established
  my steps...*
  Your circumstances, like David's, may be so se-
  vere that there is no stability, no foundation
  on which to stand, but there is a *rock that the
  builder rejected, the Rock, Christ Jesus.* (Matthew
  21:42) You may feel despondent, vulnerable,
  and even out of control, but know that you are
  secure on the Rock, Christ Jesus.

- ◆ *He has given me a new song to sing...*
  Not only have I found a reason for a song, but
  He has given me a new song. Why a new song?
  It is because up to this point no song that has
  ever been sung before would be adequate for
  this occasion, so God in His mercy and grace
  intervened with a new song. This new song
  gave musical expression to exactly what this
  occasion calls for.

- ◆ *Praise to our God...*
  Praise is an integral part of our deliverance and
  it must be about Him and focused on who He

is. *"Bless the LORD, O my soul; And all that is within me, bless His holy name!"* (Psalm 103:1)

♦ *Many will see it and fear, and will trust in the LORD.*

Yes, this is the testimony when many will see what he has done and be astounded.

During this time I remembered a cassette recording of praise music that a friend had sent to me. I found it and put it in my little recorder. I had never heard such music. The song, *Arise and sing, ye children of Zion for the Lord has delivered thee,* became my theme. It began to transform my feelings of utter frustration and despair to rays of hope. No, it wasn't easy but I CHOSE TO PRAISE! I purchased a little dual cassette player and with it I made copies for my bathroom and my kitchen. When I would get into my car and despair would try to roll in, I would hit that play button and I would *Arise and Sing!* When I would get up in the morning and the overwhelming reality of my circumstances was like a mighty wave, I would *Arise and Sing!* I took it literally! It became the Word of the Lord to me and when all other words failed, this praise music lifted me into another realm of faith and trust in God. It became my

> *"Trust in the LORD with all your heart, and lean not on your own understanding; in all your ways acknowledge Him, and He shall direct your paths."*

bridge over troubled water and the light at the end of my tunnel.

I choose to praise. Heb 13:15 says, *"By him therefore let us offer the sacrifice of praise to God continually, that is, the fruit of our lips giving thanks to his name."* Yes, Lord, I will offer myself as a living sacrifice to you and praise you the more. (Roman 12:1)

When things looked impossible, I began to speak affirmations from the Word of God. In the face of overwhelming discouragement I began to make declarations of faith.

Lord, I feel out of control. How do I move on?

"Trust in the LORD with all your heart,
and lean not on your own understanding;
in all your ways acknowledge Him,
and He shall direct your paths."
(Proverbs 3:5-6)

"I WILL ENDURE!"

What about my children? They are just embarking on their marriages and their ministries.

How can they overcome this disappointment and rejection?

"For He shall give His angels charge over you,
to keep you in all your ways."

Lord, I commit them to the safekeeping
of the Holy Spirit and the angels.

"I WILL ENDURE!"

How will I live? I had been left with no financial support.

"My God shall supply all your need according to His riches in glory by Christ Jesus."

"I WILL ENDURE!"

I feel humiliated and disgraced. What do I do with my calling? Where do I fit?

A few friends responded with concern but the religious agenda in my circle was one of suspicion and judgment. I had been taught that if ministers had major problems – it was over! Just take down your ministry shingle and call it quits. 2 Timothy 1:9 *"who has saved us and called us with a holy calling, not according to our works, but according to His own purpose and grace which was given to us in Christ Jesus before time began."* Hebrews 13:5-6 says, *"For He Himself has said, 'I will never leave you nor forsake you.' So we may boldly say: 'The LORD is my helper; I will not fear. What can man do to me?'"*

One evening, when the emotional pain was so intense that my very bones ached and my chest felt as though it was on fire, I fell to the floor in utter exhaustion and there I had one of the greatest encounters with the Holy Spirit I have ever had. At that moment I received a revelation of God's hands extended toward me as if to hand me something. Written on one hand was *GRACE* and the other hand was *MERCY*. When I looked more thoroughly I could see His hands pushing past all the years of hurt, pain and disappointment. I stood up with a new assurance that the same God I had met as a child and who had called me into the ministry, now was inviting me to *"come without fear, hesitation or reservation to His throne of grace, (favor) and obtain all the mercy and grace (all the forgiveness and favor) that I needed when I needed it."* (Hebrews 4:16)

"I WILL ENDURE!"

When is this going to change? Have I been denied?

The Apostle Paul faced a recurring problem or test and he referred to it as a "thorn." *"And lest I should be exalted above measure by the abundance of the revelations, a thorn in the flesh was given to me, a messenger of satan to buffet me, lest I be exalted above measure."* (2 Corinthians 12:7)

There has been a lot of speculation and even argument as to what the thorn was. I believe that we have missed what is really the greater revelation here. When you pray, God does answer but there is often an element of delay and sometimes even the element of denial. You don't hear many sermons on denial but that is exactly what Paul experienced. Here we see Paul's persistence when he says, *"concerning this thing I pleaded with the Lord three times that it might depart from me."* (2 Corinthians 12:8) But it did not depart.

Many of us can empathize with Paul because most of us have prayed a prayer and nothing seemed to be happening, or worse yet we were denied our request. But if we will submit to God's greater revelation we will understand as Paul did that something greater was at work here. *"And He said to me, 'My grace is sufficient for you, for My strength is made perfect in weakness.' Therefore most gladly I will rather boast in my infirmities, that the power of Christ may rest upon me. Therefore I take pleasure in infirmities, in reproaches, in needs, in persecutions, in distresses, for Christ's sake. For when I am weak, then I am strong."* (2 Corinthians 12:9-10)

> *God's word tells us that even if the thing we are earnestly praying for does not change or is not removed, it can be of greater value to us than the direct answer to our prayer.*

This whole text is beautiful in one sense but at the same time seems to be filled with contradiction. How can we boast in infirmities? How can we have joy when then Lord delays or denies the very thing that we think can be to our advantage?

It may be hard to believe but God's word tells us that even if the thing we are earnestly praying for does not change or is not removed, it can be of greater value to us than the direct answer to our prayer. Barnes Notes says that *the removal of the problem might be apparently a blessing, but it might also be attended with danger to our spiritual welfare; the grace imparted may be of permanent value and may be connected with the development of some of the loveliest traits of Christian character.*

Could it be that God purposely orchestrates delay or denial? Yes! I believe that God is saying, I have a bigger agenda! I have a higher purpose and plan for you. This time of delay could be expressly designed for our benefit. You must remember God is more interested in you than he is your ministry, so the benefits of delay serve on many levels for our good.

Paul did receive an answer, not necessarily the one he wanted. He received something much more valuable: *"My grace is sufficient for you, for <u>My strength is made perfect in weakness."</u>* The lesson here is that God's strength (His grace) will have its complete manifestation in our weakest moments. Then the greater purpose will be manifest and He will be glorified! *God says, "I want to stretch and develop your faith – and in doing so you will learn that my grace is sufficient – for every situation and at all times."* Could it be that God has a divine strategy we can't always predict?

As president of **Faith Christian University**, I meet many students that desire to be in ministry; however, most of them have no concept of the journey. I often say that God is not raising "play-boys" and "play-girls" but God is developing men and women for the Kingdom. Having experienced and walked through God's divine strategy of grace, I enjoy teaching our Bible school students the divine principles of delay.

We see that, rather than being delivered, the Lord required Paul also to be faced with delay in order for him to experience *the sufficiency of God's grace.* An astounding key to this story is found in 2 Corinthians 12:10, *"I take pleasure in infirmities, in reproaches, in needs, in persecutions, in distresses, for Christ's sake. For when I am weak, then I am strong."*

Here we see Paul not only accepting the plan and purpose of God but also grasping the full revelation of grace to come to full manifestation in his life. In every one of Paul's letters he gave the same opening: *"Grace be unto you, and peace, from God our Father, and the Lord Jesus Christ."* This was just not an opening statement, I believe he had received such a profound revelation of grace that it was at the forefront of everything he did and everything he said.

In mentoring his spiritual son, Timothy, he said, *"You therefore, my son, be strong in the grace that is in Christ Jesus."* (2 Tim 2:1) This was not a casual statement but an admonition to pursue grace by making it a priority in life and ministry.

"I WILL ENDURE!"

Lord, how long? I feel like I am in an endurance race. I am weak, vulnerable.

James 4:6 says, *"But He gives more grace. Therefore He says: 'God resists the proud, but gives grace to the humble.'"*

"I WILL ENDURE!"

Lord, I am being criticized! What they are saying is not true! No one understands. How can I defend myself?

One of the hardest steps in this race of endurance is dealing with trying to establish your own defense. When accusations come, your first "knee jerk" reaction is to rush out with great gusto and say, *"No, that's not me! Here's my heart – please don't believe what you hear!"*

Psalms 84:11 brings us this good news, *"For Jehovah God is our Light and our **Protector**. **He gives us grace and glory.**"* Whatever disappointment, rejection and life-altering situation you have gone through, the Word of God declares: *you will endure!*

II Thessalonians 2:16-17 says *"Now may our Lord Jesus Christ Himself, and our God and Father, who has loved us and given us everlasting consolation and **good hope by grace, comfort your hearts and establish you in every good word and work.**"*

Friends, believe this verse with your whole heart and allow the process of activating all the grace that you need to begin to take effect in your life! Your situation is not too big! It's not too bad! It's not too strong! Instead, grab on to the Word of God and say:

I WILL ENDURE!

CHAPTER 6

Grace Is More Than Enough

One of the classes I teach at *Faith Christian University* is *Acts of the Holy Spirit*. I always look forward to studying Luke's account of the history of the early church because it's more than history; this book is a manual for every Christian Church.

Jesus said in Luke 24:49, *"I will send the Holy Spirit, just as my Father promised. But stay here in the city until the Holy Spirit comes and fills you with power from heaven."* This was the beginning of the manifestation of the power of the Holy Spirit to take the gospel to the world. The Holy Spirit from that day forward, was evident in power, joy, miracles, signs, wonders, and as we will see, the key manifestation – GRACE. *"And with great power the apostles gave witness to the resurrection of the Lord Jesus. **And great grace was upon them all.**"* (Acts 4:33)

Grace became their best advertisement! If they had had billboards I believe they would have read, *"Great grace resides here!"* What was this grace? It was the favor and blessing of God manifested in the life and ministry of every believer.

Acts chapter 11 reports a great revival that was sweeping through the city of Antioch, the largest city in the Roman Empire, a city full of pagan worship. This revival sent shock waves through the mother church in Jerusalem. To investigate this outpouring, the leaders sent Barnabas, a trusted apostle. The scripture says it was immediately clear to Barnabas that this was indeed a Holy Spirit revival because the *grace of God* was manifested, and that made him very glad. What was the criterion? GRACE! I am sure there was much excitement and enthusiasm and many gifts were in operation, but Barnabas found the evidence he was looking for: GRACE.

The beginning of this first independent Gentile congregation in Antioch marks a shift from a Jewish fellowship in Jerusalem to a Gentile Church at Antioch, and becoming a universal community. How powerful is this grace!

Another phenomenon of the early church was that as persecution spread, grace accelerated. While most people would run away from persecution and hard times, we find the apostles running toward imminent danger.

In Acts chapter 16, when Paul and Silas were on their way to a prayer meeting, they encountered the demon possessed slave girl. She and her cohorts began to follow Paul and Silas, evidently to take advantage of the crowd that would come to hear them. When Paul determined that it was time to act, he turned and cast the demon out of her. As a result a huge uproar ensued and Paul and Silas were mercilessly stripped, beaten and thrown into prison.

"But at midnight Paul and Silas were praying and singing hymns to God, and the prisoners were listening to them. Suddenly there was a great earthquake, so that the foundations of the prison were shaken; and immediately all the doors were opened and everyone's chains were loosed." (Acts 16:25-26)

For many readers this a very familiar story, but so often in our reading of scripture we skip over the details that point out the greatest manifestations of grace. From the very beginning of their imprisonment we see *grace that is more than enough.* The fact that Paul and Silas had begun to worship and turn their 'pain into gain' is nothing short of grace. The earthquake is the supernatural manifestation of the grace and favor of God. The jailer, seeing that they were loosed, cried out for this same grace to be bestowed upon him, and his entire household. That very night, they were all saved and baptized. That is profound grace!

Take note of this; upon their release, Paul and Silas were definitely aware of the imminent danger that continued to surround them – BUT GRACE WAS COMPELLING THEM TO PUT THEIR LIVES IN FURTHER DANGER AND FOLLOW

THE PASSION OF THEIR CALLING! That is *grace that is more than enough*!

Over and over we read that even though the apostles and the believers knew that the more they preached, the more opposition would rise against them, they continued to put their lives on the line and spread the gospel. Acts 9:31 tells us *"the churches throughout all Judea, Galilee, and Samaria had peace and were edified. And walking in the fear of the Lord and in the comfort of the Holy Spirit, they were multiplied."* That's grace!

Paul admonishes the church to not just continue, but **abound** in grace! Abound means to have enough — and more to spare! Increase, over and above, be in excess, to excel, have more, and have abundance! *"So we urged Titus, that as he had begun, so he would also **complete this grace in you as well**. But as you **abound** in everything — in faith, in speech, in knowledge, in all diligence, and in your love for us — see that you **abound in this grace** also. And God is able to make **all grace abound toward you**, that you, always having all sufficiency in all things, may have an abundance for every good work."* (2 Corinthians 9:8)

This same verse in The Living Bible says, *"No matter what you are going through God is able to make it up to you by giving you everything you need and more so that there will not only be enough for your own needs but plenty left over to give joyfully to others."*

The Amplified Bible gives us even more understanding, *"And God is able to make ALL GRACE (every favor and earthly blessing) come to you in abundance, so that you may always and under all circumstances and whatever the need be self-sufficient (possessing enough to require no aid or support and furnished in abundance for every good work and charitable donation)."*

There came a time in my life when I came face to face with grace. I had to decide: Am I going to indulge my emotions and allow self-pity to consume me, or am I going to agree with God and go with **abounding** grace?

I made the decision! I will agree with God! It didn't come easily; and it didn't happen overnight. It was a process walked out each day.

> *"God does not have a closed hand toward us and neither does he have a clinched fist."*

After much soul searching, I began to confess that *every favor and earthly blessing is coming to me in abundance and I will always, no matter the circumstances, have more than enough to do everything that God leads me to do.*

There are two major things that can keep us from *having more than enough.* The first is *unbelief.* We must face our unbelief! Don't be in denial. Simply say, *"Lord, I believe, help thou my unbelief."* (Mark 9:24)

The second reason might come as a surprise but I believe that *pride* is a great hindrance. However, pride is really a byproduct of unbelief. James 4:6 says that *"God resists the proud, but gives grace to the humble."* You must lay your agenda down and let God be God even in those times that you feel out of control and the most vulnerable. I believe the Holy Spirit is saying,

"If you will lay it down, I will pick you up." As long as we fight our own battles, unbelief and pride will be rampant, but when we run up the white flag and surrender, God takes over and *grace abounds.*

REMEMBER: *God does not have a closed hand toward us and neither does he have a clinched fist.* This means that God is not stingy and neither is He angry! God is generous and grace is the generosity of God! Ephesians 1:7, 8 says *"In Him we have redemption through His blood, the forgiveness of sins, according to the riches of His grace, which He made to abound toward us in all wisdom and prudence."* God has provided through His Son, redemption, forgiveness, peace, joy, and prosperity. His generosity is in abundance and the Bible says His grace is abounding toward us.

There is nothing that God desires to withhold from His children, quite the contrary; *"God is a rewarder! But without faith it is impossible to please Him, for he who comes to God must believe that He is, and that He is a rewarder of those who diligently seek Him."* (Hebrews 11:6) If God is a rewarder then there must be a reward.

Recently I was at a social occasion visiting with a lady minister and she began to relate to me all the pastors that she knew who were having all kinds of church and marital problems. I probed as to why there were problems and she was quick to let me know that it was due to the hardships of ministry. I began to ask some questions but she interrupted me again and adamantly began to tell me how the devil was targeting ministers and their families. She went on to say that they were simply trying to do the will of God but the ministry was just too hard. I certainly sympathized with her, but as she was relating her heartbreak I began to try to share what the Lord had given me several years ago.

In 1995 the Lord directed us to begin a Bible training center, which went on to become *Faith Christian University.* I began to pursue this vision with everything within me. We had tre-

> *As long we move in faith and not presumption, all the grace we need will be available to us to accomplish ANY TASK God is leading us to do.*

mendous growth and with that came a lot of new ideas, so we began to diversify and offer a lot of different programs. During the first few years, I thought every good idea was a God idea; however, I began to experience a lot of anxiety and stress. I began to have sleepless nights and would get frustrated at the least little thing. I began to lose the joy that I once had and decisions became extremely tedious. The weight of day-to-day administration began to feel all-consuming. As I assessed and evaluated the situation, I heard the Lord speak to me and say, *"Faith, my yoke is easy and my burden is light."* At once I took issue with that and reminded the Lord that I was busy doing His work. However, He said again, *"My yoke is easy and my burden is light."* Then He added, *"Faith, evidently you have yoked up with something that is not of me because if I gave it to you there would be sufficient grace to enable you to do it. So therefore, if it's too much then I didn't give it to you."* That set me back and I could not wait to open my Bible and begin to research. Yes, there it was in Matthew 11:30, *"For My yoke is easy and My burden is light."*

> **Grace is promised to be there in abundance as our faith makes it available. (Romans 5:1,2)**

I shared with my friend how that very day I began to re-evaluate what God had mandated us to do and I realized that I had moved beyond the bounds of my faith and His grace. I made some cancellations, I resigned a position and I even closed down several projects. I purposed that I would only commit to what I knew the Holy Spirit was directing us to do.

I then remembered a great book that I had read years before by Dr. Fred Price called *Faith, Foolishness or Presumption*. At that point I realized that if I expected *sufficient grace* to be available then I must move in faith, not foolishness and definitely not in presumption. And where is satan? My friend, we give him access when we move in presumption. Satan doesn't have any secret devices, no special weapons of mass destruction. He is still the 'father of liars' and he is using the same tactics that he has always used. As long as we move in faith and not presumption *all the grace we need for today and tomorrow will be available to us to accomplish ANY TASK God is leading us to do.*

There are many ministers that are needlessly suffering from stress and anxiety. They need to come to an understanding of the doctrine of *the abundance of grace.* You cannot over-extend yourself in areas where God has not led you and then presume that adequate grace will be there. Grace is promised to be there in abundance as our faith makes it available. (Romans 5:1,2) We don't presume something and then expect God's grace to bail us out. Quite the opposite! Our faith is the open door to all the grace we need – *in abundance and abounding toward us.*

I am convinced that the problem is not the ministry. I have met so many people through the years that have the wrong perception of ministry, and this wrong perception leads to presumption. Here are some guidelines I feel the Lord gave me to keep from falling into presumption:

♦ *Ask yourself, "Would I be happy doing anything else?" Know that you know that God has called you. If He has called you then grace that is 'more than enough' will accompany that call.*

♦ *Pursue your call as He directs. No matter what others are doing, remember God has specifically called you and you are like no other. Move out only in the areas that you know God has directed you.*

♦ *Make your vision and mission clear to yourself, your family and those you are called to. Pray every day over your vision and don't be afraid to speak it out. Don't allow someone else to dictate your call – only the Holy Spirit.*

♦ *Walk out your calling in faith knowing that grace will be there in abundance to pursue whatever God directs you to do.*

♦ *Purpose that you will not be motivated by pride and fall into presumption and foolishness.*

> *...we must serve by inspiration not by imitation.* ఇ

I urge our *FCU* students to be careful and not move out presumptuously, but instead, realize that ministry must be Spirit led, not pride motivated. We are not in competition with one another and we must *serve by inspiration not by imitation.*

Over the years I have watched people with a heart to serve the Lord fall into a trap of presumption and go into excess debt, putting a strain on the church, their ministry and even their marriage. If your vision is from God it won't destroy your marriage or your church. It won't cause you to lose your children. God has promised His grace in abundance when He calls you into the ministry. *"And I thank Christ Jesus our Lord who has enabled me, because He counted me faithful, **putting me into the ministry, and the grace of our Lord was exceedingly abundant, with faith and love** which are in Christ Jesus."* (1 Timothy 1:12,14)

We can learn so much from Paul's life and ministry. He states over and over that the Lord *"called me by His grace"* and not only his calling, but also his effectiveness, was directly related to GRACE. *"I became a minister **according to the gift of the grace of God** given* *to me by the effective working of His power."* (Ephesians 3:7) Paul also states that this grace was recognizable and imparted to others. *"James, Cephas, and John, who seemed to be pillars, perceived the grace that had been given to me."* (Galatians 2:9)

Paul brings an understanding that we are all called and all the grace we need is available to us. *"But to each one of us grace was given according to the measure of Christ's gift."* (Ephesians 4:7) Grace provided the power and equipment for his ministry. *"Through Him we have received grace and apostleship for obedience to the faith among all nations for His name."* (Romans 1:5) Paul said that he was an apostle because he had received *"apostolic grace."* He didn't call himself – God called him so therefore he knew that the evidence of an apostle or any other gifting is not established in a title but in the effectiveness of his call.

In other words, if there is no grace you have moved without the bounds of your calling or you may not be called at all. Paul says that if you operate in your gifting and calling there will be plenty of grace – grace that is more than enough – abounding toward you. However, the tendency is to presume and manufacture success. It may feel like the real thing and sometimes even look like the real thing, but if you are operating in the flesh; you will end up with a fleshly imitation!

> *...the evidence of an apostle or any other gifting is not established in a title but in the effectiveness of his call.*

We see in 1 Corinthians 3:10 that Paul was *restricted* by the grace of God that was given to him. *"According to the grace of God which was given to me."* I would rather say that he restricted himself by not presuming and stepping out foolishly and calling it "faith."

Hebrews 12:28, says *"Therefore, since we are receiving a kingdom, which cannot be shaken, **let us have grace, by which we may serve God acceptably with reverence and godly fear."***

Remember: Grace gives access to your calling and abounds to whatever degree to which you need it. God may lead you into full time ministry or call you to serve in a secular career. It makes no difference; His grace is sufficient and more than enough!

- Grace is God's power being released into your life.
- Grace is God's power enabling you to perform supernatural ministry.
- Grace is GOD'S ABILITY!
- Grace gives birth to ALL ministry gifts.

I believe a secret for Paul was that he labored in conjunction with grace and he did not lay claim to any of the fruit, in fact, he was quick to say, *"But by the grace of God I am what I am, and His grace toward me was not in vain; but I labored more abundantly than they all, yet not I, but the grace of God which was with me."* (1 Corinthians 15:10)

There will be times when God will stretch your faith. You may be called upon to expand your vision and take yourself out of your comfort zone and even beyond your capability. So what is the criterion? Know this, that grace can multiply and grow and it will be there in accordance with the task. Grace that is more than enough.

"May Grace and peace be multiplied to you in the knowledge of God and of Jesus our Lord."
(2 Peter 1:2)

✽ *Family* ✽

CHAPTER 7

Grace Is Access

Today, everywhere you turn, someone or something is asking for your access code. We must include in our daily lives a myriad of passwords, pin numbers and code words necessary to transact business in every venue from bank accounts, credit cards, debit cards, computers, phones, emails and websites. This requirement is designed to give me, the possessor of the code, *access* to whatever transaction I need to conduct. Access is a very important word in our lives.

In regard to our spiritual life, it means everything. Many people, even Christians, still struggle with how to gain access (entrance and admission) to God. Religion says it is a difficult, questionable and doubtful proposition, but if you're lucky, under the right set of circumstances, access to God might be granted. *My friend, access is already provided.*

Jesus said, "I am the way."
(John 14:6)

His blood is the "new and living way."
(Hebrews 10:20)

Through Him we have "access by faith
into this grace wherein we stand."
(Romans 5:2)

Through Him we both have access by
"one Spirit unto the Father."
(Ephesians 2:18)

In whom we have ... "access in
confidence, through our faith in him."
(Ephesians 3:12).

There it is – positive assurance that we have FREE
and FULL access to our Heavenly Father. I love what
the New Unger's Bible Dictionary says, *By the con-
tinuous power and efficiency of His atoning act, Jesus is
the constant Bringer to the Father.*

So when we read this scripture, *"For through Him
(Christ) we both have access by one Spirit to the Father,"*
(Ephesians 2:18) lights should go on and bells should
ring. This is incredible!

Growing up in the church, I had the perception
that anything God had was not easily accessed. The
legalist attitude of the denomination that I was in produced the perception that every scripture must pass
through our catalog of experience and be closely scru-
tinized. I was left with:

"What if.....?"

"How long.....?"

"What do I do until.....?"

"How will I live...?"

This produced a questioning mentality that developed into a complete lack of confidence in approaching God, and created a "hope so, maybe so" kind of faith. This worked okay, until times got really tough. Then I didn't have anything firm to stand on.

I, like probably many of you, knew that I had admittance but I was not fully convinced that I had full access. One day, during my family crisis, I stopped at the supermarket as I had done thousands of times before. Feeling drained of all energy, I gave myself a pep-talk: You can do this – Just go in – Get the cart...

I knew every aisle and where everything was that I needed. It was routine; however, as I began to push my cart, I became totally blank and almost disoriented, forgetting not only why I went in but actually forgetting where I was. This was very frightening. I wanted to believe that God was my *strong tower*, but I certainly wasn't experiencing it. My heart longed for the access to the all-sufficiency of God's grace that I had read about all of my life.

Well-meaning friends would tell me to "pray longer and pray harder – believe more." In other words, "Do something!" I was willing to do anything. But what was the right thing? The big question was "Where is that place of grace" and bigger yet, "How do I access it?"

Following my divorce, I became the part time music director at a great church in Orlando, Florida. I had been associated with this church for many years and the pastor was a very close friend. He called me one day to say that he wanted to introduce me to a gentleman in the church. I immediately revolted and told him I was definitely not interested; however, after a series of chance events we came face to face. I immediately knew he was very different from anyone I'd been around. When I met Bud Fredrick I was still in a recuperative state from the divorce, and was dealing with a lot of anger. From our first meeting he exuded optimism and faith, and began to pour hope and restoration into me. He had an answer for everything I was going through and it all spelled F-A-I-T-H. After just a few weeks he began to talk marriage and it scared me to death, but within a few months, and with our pastor's blessing, we were married.

Immediately he began to encourage me to attend *Rhema Bible Training Center*, where he had graduated from a few years earlier. We soon moved to Tulsa, Oklahoma. It was not an easy transition because I had already been in ministry for many years and was now starting over by attending Bible School. I quickly began to realize I was being brought not only into deeper knowledge of the Word of God, but to a new place of "knowing" and a lifestyle of faith.

Knowing your Heavenly Father is the key to understanding and accessing the grace of God!

After a few months at *Rhema* I remember thinking, "What do I really *know*? Do I know doubt and unbelief more than I know He whom I have believed in?" I ask you the same question, "What do you *know*?"

Do you know...

JEHOVAH JIREH – MY PROVIDER

This is the name that Abraham ascribed to God for providing the ram for sacrifice, saving his son, Isaac. (Genesis 22:14)

Do you know...

JEHOVAH NISSI – MY BANNER

When Israel defeated the Amalekites, Moses signified this victory by building an altar and named it The Lord is My Banner. (Exodus 17:15)

Do you know...

JEHOVAH-SHALOM – PRINCE OF PEACE

This Name of God is based on the incredible story of Gideon and the miraculous victory that God brought forth in Judges 6:11-23. The unbelievable words spoken to Gideon by the Angel of the Lord, *"The LORD is with you, you mighty man of valor!"* This is not the way Gideon would have characterized himself. While his mind swirled with questions and reservations he asked, *"O my lord, if the LORD is with us, why then has all this happened to us?"* Without having all the answers, Gideon opened his heart and accessed the grace necessary to do what God commissioned him to do.

Paul writes in Romans 5:1,2 *"Therefore, having been justified by faith, we have peace with God through our Lord Jesus Christ, through whom also we have <u>access by faith into this grace</u> in which we stand, and rejoice in hope of the glory of God."*

Romans 5:2 holds the key. ***Need grace? Step into faith!*** Faith is more than mental assent. Faith is more than just saying, *"Lord I believe."* Faith is based on *knowing*. It is a confidence – not a stab in the dark! Faith has substance and that substance is in *knowing*. As I continued to grow in the knowledge of the Word of God, my faith began to accelerate and I had the access code: **Knowing your Heavenly Father is the key to understanding and accessing the grace of God!**

> *All the grace and favor of God is available if we will step through the door of faith and access it.*

Even the simplest of Bible stories took on new meaning as I studied and began to see God's faithfulness in a new light. Sometimes it was through a song, sometimes through a sermon, but always in unexpected ways. Noah, Abraham, Moses, the children of Israel, David and on and on. I began to see a pattern of trust and grace.

In the New Testament Jesus' very own words establish that to build our faith and access the grace, we must know who Jesus is. Jesus said, *"I am the way and the truth and the life. No one comes to the Father except through me."* (John 14:6) In John 10:7, *"I tell you the truth, I am the gate for the sheep."* In verse 9, *"I am the gate; whoever enters through me will be saved."* There is no access to God other than through Jesus Christ. Our salvation is by and through faith in the blood of Jesus and thereby we gain *"access"* into the very throne room of God. *We must believe that Jesus is the way – and there is no other way.*

Many believers are still seeking other resources to accomplish and access what the Lord Jesus has already made available to us in His Word. Your search should be over. It's not necessary to seek another word, another way or another person – Jesus has gained us 'access' into the very heart of God.

In 1 Peter 3:18, we see that the Apostle Peter has left his sphere of doubt and now has come to a thorough understanding of not only what Jesus suffered, but more importantly "why" He suffered. Christ died to bring you to God! Peter is so clearly saying that Christ's death and resurrection was to bring you to God and give you "access" to everything He has promised, BUT you must believe. Jesus bought and paid for our ability to come to God. Don't deny yourself this beautiful privilege.

All the grace and favor of God is available if we will step through the door of faith and *access* it. Know this, that while we are struggling and asking the:

> *"What if…..?"*
> > *"How long…..?"*
> > > *"What do I do until…..?"*
> > > > *"How will I live…?"*

God has already provided complete and perfect *access* to everything He has, but it can only be accessed – made available – and received as we step through the door of faith.

**Grace is that ingredient that follows FAITH.
FAITH precedes GRACE.**

Even though the Apostle Paul did not have the privilege of being one of Jesus' disciples, the revelation He received following his conversion set the precedent. We see him emerging with astounding revelation of unwavering faith and confidence to access all the grace he needs for his life and ministry. In Hebrews 4:15-16, *"For we do not have a high priest who is unable to sympathize with our weaknesses, but we have one who has been tempted in every way, just as we are – yet was without sin. Let us then approach the throne of grace with confidence, so that we may receive mercy and find grace to help us in our time of need."*

Again he steps forward in Ephesians 3:12, 13, declaring that *"in whom we have boldness and access with confidence through faith in Him. Therefore I ask that you do not lose heart at my tribulations for you, which is your glory."* This is amazing! Paul then sums it up by saying in Galatians 3:14, *"the blessing of Abraham (the unmerited favor of God) might come on the Gentiles through Jesus Christ; that we might receive the promise of the Spirit through faith."*

We see faith in action. Faith accelerates = grace. Faith is the catalyst of grace! God always provides access to whatever He promises. With God there are no "hidden agendas" or "spiritual surprises." His Word is ever true. If God says it,

> **Grace is that ingredient that follows FAITH.** ❦

you can believe it. It is no wonder that Paul said, *"And not only that, but we also glory in tribulations, knowing that tribulation produces perseverance; and perseverance, character; and character, hope. Now hope does not disappoint, because the love of God has been poured out in our hearts by the Holy Spirit who was given to us."* (Romans 5:3-5)

Paul states over and over, "Yes, you will go through things – nothing you can do will change that; however, God is more concerned about the way you go through it than the contortions we put ourselves through to try to change it.

Faith gives access to grace!

Faith is the door into this grace!

Faith is our extended hand toward God!

Grace is God's extended hand toward us.

You will find all the help, provision, anointing, and power – everything you need – at the throne of grace. Please hear me! In my time of crisis my own preconceived ideas and speculations of how and what God must do were useless to me. I found that He did not need my permission or my ideas for good to come out of this situation.

Anxiety will blind you. If doesn't blind you it will definitely distract you. Either way it is all designed to rob you of your ability to focus on your faith and access the grace you need. The accessibility of grace is obvious! It's clear! Grace brings about the desired result but it's only by and through faith. Here is what I discovered:

Grace answers… "What if…?"

Grace answers… "How long…?"

Grace answers… "What do I do until…?"

Grace answers… "How will I live…?"

CHAPTER 8

Grace Is Whoever

*L*ights! Camera! Action!

Okay, so maybe it was more like amateur hour, but every Christmas season my little home church looked forward to our traditional presentation of the Christmas Story. There wasn't a lot of enthusiasm among the congregation generated by the "arts" so, when I was 14 years old I became the producer, director, and chief musician for our simple rendition. Each year we would select three little boys for shepherds, three tall older boys for wise men, and, of course, a Mary and Joseph. Then there was the role coveted by every little girl: the angel.

On that special night, as the little characters hovered around the manger scene at stage left, the three little shepherd boys would take their positions at stage right. The light would go on and the shepherds would stand back with amazement as the angel proclaimed, *"Do not be afraid, for behold, I bring you good tidings of great joy which will be to <u>all people</u>."* (Luke 2:10)

There it was! Our declaration of faith – that Jesus came to ALL PEOPLE. If someone had stood up and demanded, "DEFINE ALL PEOPLE" it would have seemed ridiculous because there it was simply and directly stated: ALL PEOPLE!

On any Sunday morning our tiny congregation could be heard singing *"Amazing Grace," "Love Lifted Me"* and *"What can wash away my sins? Nothing but the blood of Jesus!"* Every Sunday the children sang, *"Jesus loves the little children, all the children of the world, red, and yellow, black and white, they are precious in His sight, Jesus loves the little children of the world."* Like most churches, we proudly proclaimed WHOEVER!

Our denomination was very devoted to foreign missions, and several times each year a missionary would come to show slides, tell stories, and inform us about their ministry overseas. I remember the stories of the heathen in some far distant country. My, how we would rejoice when the missionary explained how they had received Christ. We were quick to respond in offerings because we believed that everyone had a right to hear the Gospel.

Early in my childhood I remember one particular Sunday night that the church was filled with the saints shouting, singing and worshiping God. All of a sudden I had the feeling that we were being watched. I turned my little head (I probably was standing up in the pew) and peered out the window to see black faces peering back at me. To my surprise they looked like the same folks that were in the missionary's pictures. Their expressions emanated the same joy of the Lord, and some were even clapping with the music, and singing along. It was a beautiful sight. You could see that they were no strangers to what the Spirit of God was doing in our midst, but they knew "their place." Word had spread about the anointed music and preaching, and the hunger for the Spirit drew them. They were 'saints' just like us and everybody knew it, but they were not invited to join us in worship.

This confused me. I couldn't reconcile this picture because, as Pentecostals, we understood what it meant to be ostracized and not accepted into the mainstream. We had felt the sting of prejudice. Our church was housed in an old frame building located across the railroad tracks, with no air-conditioning, no padded pews and no impressive lobby. Being Pentecostal was not in style and was often misunderstood. Our little church was the object of jokes and scorn. I remember the sickening feeling I had when I overheard my girlfriend's mother refer to our family as "holy rollers" and "tongue talkers." I would have thought the shared experience of being misjudged would bring a common ground, however, we were perpetrating the same lack of acceptance and prejudice on other believers who happened to be a different color. We were all believers – so what was the problem? We sang the songs and presented the image of acceptance, but that was as far as it went. According to our own statement of beliefs we were supposed to be the church of "whoever." With the windows opened wide, the music and singing would fill the air as if to say, "Everyone is welcome." But it simply wasn't true. Everyone wasn't welcome.

Growing up in the Deep South in the 1950's, racial prejudice, bigotry and hatred filled each thread of everyday life. The racial prejudice and tension that ran through the very core of this small town did not stop at the *Five and Dime* or the segregated public schools, but boldly took up residence in our churches. One day our little "Christian" town and even my home church were put to the test. The story goes that a young black man had made a flirtatious remark to a young white woman coming out of the *A&P Grocery* store. The young woman went home and told her husband, who in turn passed the word to his friends. The following morning, news quickly spread and the town was abuzz that "this young black man had met his proper punishment and was in the local hospital." Those responsible were arrested and interrogated but soon released. The news was that even some "good deacons" were involved.

There was no outcry from the churches. The ministerial association was silent because some of the perpetrators were officers in the church. I remember going to bed so frightened because there were threats of reprisal from both sides. Finally the Federal Government intervened, but rumors continued to fly and there was a spirit of unrest. The true crime was never discussed.

Sadly, the history of the Christian church is filled with stories of bigotry and hatred involving every conceivable level of prejudice. Our sermons and songs have proclaimed a gospel of "whoever" but most importantly, what do we practice?

Everything from color, race, hairstyle, outward adornment, social status and geography – you name it – has divided the church of the Lord Jesus Christ. Grace has been withheld based on the most frivolous of reasons, and on the most ridiculous of excuses. Grace is truly on trial.

> *"Whoever calls on the name of the LORD shall be saved." Joel 2:32*

The Prophet Joel said, *"Whoever calls on the name of the LORD shall be saved."* (Joel 2:32) and it is repeated in Acts 2:21 as well as Romans 10:13. Jesus said in Luke 10:2-12, *"The harvest truly is great, but the laborers are few; therefore pray the Lord of the harvest to send out laborers into His harvest."* What color is the harvest? Is it male or female? Is poor or rich? Does it have pink hair or blond? Who did God have in mind when He said "whoever?"

For three years Peter, the fisherman, as well as the other disciples, followed Jesus and listened as He consistently instructed them as to the pattern for the harvest. Peter was there, front and center, when Jesus gave the commission in Acts 1:8 to receive the power of the Holy Spirit and become witnesses in Jerusalem, Judea, Samaria, and to the end of the earth. There was no qualifying and there were no exceptions! Witness to everybody – everywhere!

Now following the upper room outpouring of the Holy Spirit in Acts 2, we find Peter emerging, with an uncommon boldness, and anointed of the Holy Spirit. As he steps forth to deliver a dynamic message of salvation to the thousands of people gathered in Jerusalem, there is no doubt that he was called to be an apostle. If we follow Peter we see him fully engaged in supernatural ministry. However, in order to fulfill his calling, the Holy Spirit begins to invade an area in Peter's life that I believe takes him by complete surprise.

God can work through anything but He can only work in a person who is totally yielded to Him. ✍

It begins in Acts chapter 10 with a man named Cornelius, a Roman centurion, whom the Bible refers to as a devout and God fearing man. Even though he is a Roman, a heathen, an enemy of Israel, the Bible says 'an angel of the Lord' came to him and instructed him to pursue a man called Peter. At this same time Peter, being a very devout Jew, went up on the roof to pray. While there, he became hungry and began making preparation to eat. He fell into a trance or open vision and saw a sheet come down full of four-footed animals, reptiles and birds. The angel instructs Peter to kill and eat it, however, Peter was horrified. As a Jew, these types of animals were considered unclean and should not be eaten. He loudly protested, not once, but three separate times. Acts 10:15 records, *"The voice spoke to him again, 'Do not call anything impure that God has made clean.'"* Peter was still contemplating the vision when a knock came at his door. The Spirit gave him a command and said that he was not to ask questions or hesitate but go with the men that Cornelius had sent. This was quite a feat for a man who had just received a very perplexing vision. At this point I believe Peter began to realize that the Holy Spirit was definitely at work. God can work *through* anything but He can only work *in* a person who is totally yielded to Him. The calling and destiny that God had planned for Peter demanded that he deal with his prejudice.

Once in Cornelius' house Peter made it clear that, even though as a Jew it was unlawful for him to be there, God had revealed a greater truth. *"Then Peter opened his mouth and said: 'In truth I perceive that God shows no partiality. But in every nation whoever fears Him and works righteousness is accepted by Him. The word which God sent to the children of Israel, preaching peace through Jesus Christ – He is Lord of all.'"* (Acts 10:34-36)

Over the next few days Peter preached and ministered to these "uncircumcised" Romans and many were saved, filled with the Spirit and baptized in water. What a drastic change! In Acts 10, the future of the early church was at stake, and Peter's admission of prejudice cleared the way for the church to follow in the words of Jesus, *"Go into all the world and preach the gospel to EVERY CREATURE."* (Mark 16:15) Because of Peter's obedience, the back of prejudice had been revealed and broken that day.

So many Churches are separated and divided over the *gospel of grace.* Some believe that unless you are baptized into their particular church or participate in some special formula that they have implemented – your salvation is in vain. Why is it that the Bible clearly states "whoever" and yet some feel it necessary to invent requirements to the grace of God based upon a few opinions and preferences?

One Sunday morning, shortly after we began pastoring our first church in Montgomery Alabama, I was sent to monitor a new Sunday School Class. I approached the classroom just in time to hear the teacher announce that he was going to enlighten the class on the true origin of the black race. I could not believe my ears. This was a man that not only taught one of the main adult classes but was also a deacon. He and his entire family were regarded as "pillars of the church." I listened closely as he began to read in the book of Genesis concerning the story of Noah and his son, Ham. His version was that this story clearly revealed that the black race was doomed to servitude and God looked at them as a cursed race unworthy of redemption. My heart sank. Upon investigation we soon found that prejudice was rampant throughout the congregation.

How could we sing songs about redemption, salvation and the love of God and have prejudice and racism accepted and even encouraged? The gospel is good news and that 'good news' is for EVERYBODY, EVERYWHERE! How do I know? Because "the Bible tells me so."

But prejudice and bigotry are not only racial. They cover a wide variety of venues. In the 1970's the winds of the Holy Spirit began to blow across denominational lines, and believers in the major denominations, as well as Catholics, became "Spirit-filled" and began to speak in tongues. It sent a shock wave through our Pentecostal churches, and all our standards of holiness underwent a renovation. All of a sudden we became aware that God did not need our permission to *"pour out His Spirit upon all flesh."* (Joel 2:28) A lot of Pentecostal people and their denominations were "shook up" because we had taken comfort in our separatism and the fact that we were a "special and peculiar" people. God overrode all of our opinions and our prejudice by *pouring out His Spirit upon ALL FLESH!*

Several years later an overflow of this spiritual move swept across the young people of America and gave birth to the "Jesus People." They were full of faith and evangelism was their focus. I can remember much discussion and debate as young people moved into our congregations with long, shaggy hair, beads and strange music, but full of the love of Jesus. These non-conformists proved again that when God says all people, He means *all people.*

John 3:16-17

For God so loved the world that He gave His only begotten Son, that whoever believes in Him should not perish but have everlasting life. For God did not send His Son into the world to condemn the world, but that the world through Him might be saved.

113

♦ How will we ever convince a lost world of the love of Jesus if we cannot demonstrate that love to each other?

♦ How can we convince a morally bankrupt society that God loves ALL people if we ourselves are selective to whom we share the gospel?

♦ We have ALL sinned and are in need of a Savior, but now according to God's Word we ALL are declared justified, righteous, reconciled and restored through the blood of Jesus.

♦ IT'S CALLED GRACE.

Romans 3:23-24

"For all have sinned and fall short of the glory of God, being justified freely by His grace through the redemption that is in Christ Jesus."

Every reference to any gift, blessing, promise is overwhelmingly available to ALL!

A great story is told about the great apostle to South Africa, John G. Lake, from the biography ***A Man Without Compromise*** by Wilford Reidt. While preaching one night in South Africa, Lake asked a cherished black brother named Elias Letwaba to come to the platform. Lake put his arm around this black man and called him, *"My brother."* Some of the whites in the audience were furious! They booed and hissed.

Lake turned like a flash and shouted, "My friends, God has made of one blood all nations of men. If you do not want to acknowledge these as your brothers, then you'll have the mortification of going away into eternal woe, while you see many of these black folk going to eternal bliss. *'Whosoever hateth his brother is a murderer: and ye know that no murderer hath eternal life abiding in him"* (1 John 3:15).

Then Lake held out his hand and welcomed Letwaba. Many in the crowd were shouting and demanding that the "black devils" be put out and kicked into the street. However, Lake, with his hand still on Letwaba's shoulder, said calmly, *"If you turn out these men, then you must turn me out too, for I will stand by my black brethren."*

Such love was new to the black man and it won his heart. By the end of the meeting, the gainsayers had fallen into a sullen silence. In the beautiful way that only God can orchestrate, it was Brother Elias Letwaba who took over the work in South Africa when Apostle Lake returned to America.

I have been privileged to minister in many churches throughout South Africa for the past several years and look forward to returning. The pastors and apostles that I have met are truly special women and men that are setting the pace for a new season and a new day for this great nation. The truth is that many churches and ministries played an integral part in ending apartheid as well as praying for a peaceful transition. The gospel of Jesus Christ is a yoke-destroying, burden-removing gospel! Thank God, when put to the test it always comes through.

Jesus left us with the mandate to *"go into the world and preach the gospel to EVERY CREATURE."* (Acts 1:8) The Apostle Paul obeyed that mandate and made no distinction between any people at anytime. He continued to encourage believers to accept each other on the basis of the grace of God and not allow any prejudice of any kind to invade our lives and ministries.

> *"A new commandment I give to you, that you love one another, as I have loved you." John 13:34*

In his epistle to the Romans he states, *"Be kindly affectionate to one another with brotherly love, in honor giving preference to one another; Bless those who persecute you; bless and do not curse. Rejoice with those who rejoice, and weep with those who weep. Be of the same mind toward one another. Do not set your mind on high things, but associate with the humble. Do not be wise in your own opinion. Repay no one evil for evil. Have regard for good things in the sight of all men. If it is possible, as much as depends on you, live peaceably with all men."* (Romans 12:13 –18) This is it! This is the call! Without it we are nothing!

Jesus laid out a new commandment and it is the commandment of love as presented in John 13:34-35, *"A new commandment I give to you, that you love one another; as I have loved you, that you also love one another. By this all will know that you are My disciples, if you have love for one another."*

Grace: It is for me. It is for you. It is for whoever.

CHAPTER 9

Grace in the Church

Growing up in the Church, I always perceived it as my "safe zone." This is where we were spiritually and socially sustained. This is where we made friends and invested our lives. The church was a representation of Jesus Christ. However, there came a time in my life when what I perceived as this "safe zone" became a great disappointment. I soon became aware that my perception of what church should be was far different from what I was experiencing.

The pain of losing my marriage was hard enough, but it was extremely difficult to try to explain to my children why the church, which had been our whole life, was now strangely silent. Now that I needed critical care I quickly found out that the church that I knew and loved seemed to be unsympathetic and detached, and I felt like I was among strangers. The grace that had been preached and demonstrated for the addict, the thief, the liar and even the fornicator was now in jeopardy; there was a line drawn in the sand that said, *"Grace is under consideration."*

When Jesus spoke the words, *"I will build my church,"* as recorded in Matthew 16:18, what did He have in mind? What was He really referring to? I believe we will find the answer as we follow the pattern of the New Testament Church.

For three years twelve men followed Jesus, and during this time He endeavored to prepare them for what was to come. Then, following His death and resurrection, there were forty days of intense teaching and training. After His ascension we find that 120 responded and obeyed His word to *"go and wait in Jerusalem for the Promise of the Father."* (Acts 1:4) Just as Jesus had promised, they were all filled with the power of the Holy Spirit.

After the great outpouring, Peter stepped forward with a mandate from the Holy Sprit and preached with such unction and anointing that 3,000 people were saved! From this day forward, this small band of believers becomes the *movers and shakers* of their day. Their voice and message became so prominent that thousands were saved, healed and delivered. The Holy Spirit was manifested in streets, in homes and in the highest courts of law – all because a band of people grabbed hold of the vision and mandate of Jesus – *"I will build my church and the gates of hell will not prevail against it."* (Matthew 16:18)

As we witness this phenomenon, it's not long before very serious opposition and hatred rise up against every believer. The great Apostles of the Church, Peter and John, are soon arrested. They are released, but not without preaching a stirring, fervent message about Jesus. The church bands together and begins to pray for even more boldness, even though they knew the serious threats that were being made against them. Nothing was going to deter them from preaching the gospel and proclaiming the name of Jesus. They walked with a daring faith, preaching, caring, loving, sharing and being willing to suffer, even die for the cause of Christ.

In spite of all the threats and persecution, the favor and blessing of God, called, "grace" begins to emerge and be accessed in unprecedented ways. Evidence of this is found in Acts 4:33, which says, *"And with great power the apostles gave witness to the resurrection of the Lord Jesus. And great grace was upon them all."*

Stephen's death, as the first martyr of the church, is recorded in Acts Chapter 7, and is a tragic blow to the church. Persecution is being escalated and unleashed against the church so they begin to flee in many directions, carrying the gospel as they go. Soon news travels back to the mother church in Jerusalem of a great Holy Ghost outpouring in the Greek city of Antioch. All kinds of people are accepting Jesus as Messiah, and many miracles and strange happenings are going on. The Holy Spirit is being manifested in an unprecedented way. (Acts 11.)

Right in the face of persecution, abandonment and dispersion, the church grows stronger and multiplies in all directions. Throughout the book of Acts you will find grace present and very active in the heart of every believer and in the heart of every church. There is no doubt that the favor and blessing of God is being manifested. Grace is present.

If we, as the church, desire to walk in a profound revelation of the gospel of grace, we must follow the example of the New Testament church and we cannot ignore the evidence.

The Evidence of Obedience

The disciples had a history of being somewhat unreliable and a little noncommittal, but after Jesus had risen from the dead He gathered them together and spent 40 days teaching and investing the future of His church to this band of believers. If you read the account you will see that He gave explicit instructions that once He left, they were not to disperse but go into Jerusalem and wait for the manifestation of the power of the Holy Spirit. What that meant, they did not know; they were simply expected to obey.

Following Jesus' ascension, 120 disciples responded in complete obedience and *"joined together constantly in prayer, along with the women and Mary the mother of Jesus, and with his brothers."* (Acts 1:14) Obedience led the way to grace. Without complete obedience, faith would not have been produced, and grace could not have been accessed.

The Evidence of Unity (Oneness)

"When the day of Pentecost came, they were all together in one place." (Acts 2:1). Not splintered – not

opinionated, but in complete unity. As a result, they were all filled with the Holy Spirit and the New Testament Church was birthed. Special attention must be given to the correlation of the Holy Spirit being manifest, and the atmosphere being permeated with total unity and oneness.

This is supposed to be the church – this is the church that Jesus built. Not what some committee has deliberated over and decided fit their agenda. Not a split from another group that was born out of anger and offense – but a community of believers, birthed in love so the most lonely and desolate of heart would be warmly embraced. Then grace was manifested!

Do you want grace in your life and in your church? *"This is My commandment, that you love one another as I have loved you... Greater love has no one than this, than to lay down one's life for his friends.* (John 15:12-13) Then Jesus mandates in verse 17, *"These things I command you, that you love one another."*

> **The spirit of unity was one of the reasons that grace abounded in the church and propelled them go into all the world and preach the gospel.**

When Jesus said, in Matthew 16:18, *"I will build my church,"* I ask again, "What kind of a church would that be?" In order for the church to be the true church Jesus spoke of, we must be in **total unity and agreement.** Our pattern, our model for "oneness" is found in John 17:22, in the passionate intercession of Jesus to His Holy Father, *"make them one, as we are one."*

Unity means *harmony, agreement, accord and union.* However, you cannot have unity without agreement and you cannot have agreement without unity. The spirit of unity was one of the reasons that *grace abounded in the church* and propelled them to *go into all the world and preach the gospel.*

How can we, professing to be the New Testament Church, fulfill the mission that Jesus has given us when there is strife and division among the professing believers of the same church, much less, those of different organizations and denominations? There's disagreement in the music department, women's ministry, among the leaders and sometimes against the pastor. Yet we are singing hallelujahs, jumping, shouting and calling it worship while our hearts are divided, full of prejudice and pride.

The fruit of the church is oneness.

Matthew Henry's Commentary says:

The fruit of the church is oneness. It is evidence of the truth of Christianity, and a means of bringing many to embrace it. In general, it will recommend Christianity to the world. When Christianity, instead of causing quarrels about itself, makes all other strife's to cease,-when it disposes men to be kind and loving, anxious to preserve and promote peace, this will recommend it to all who have anything either of

122

natural religion or natural affection in them. The evidence, that of their being one: it will appear that God loves us, if we love one another with a pure heart.

The characteristic of love is what Jesus prayed would be manifested in His church. The relationship of the Father to the Son is a demonstration of

> **The Church is to be the safest place in the community and serve as an agency of love and protection.**

what the church is supposed to be as a *testimony to the world*. The degree of unity that is demonstrated upon this earth among the brethren, the world will see and know the *grace* of Almighty God. This is recorded twice in John 17:21, *"That the world may believe that you have sent me."* And again in verse 23, *"That the world may know it."* The responsibility is on our shoulders as members of the body. The mandate is clear – the banners are waving. *Great Grace resides here!*

The Evidence of Caring

The Church is to be the *safest place in the community* and serve as an agency of love and protection, fulfilling Jesus' words to the Father in John 17:1, *"I do not pray that You should take them out of the world, but that You should keep them from the evil one."* One of the chief characteristics of the early church was a sharing and caring for one another. The church must reach out beyond people's differences, faults and failures, and represent what Jesus intended, *a safe place.* Our marquees should read, "There is no judgment here, all are welcome. All are safe!" This will produce GRACE!

The Church of Jesus Christ is to be an agency of redemption, protection and restoration for every man, woman, boy and girl, regardless of color, race, social distinction, or any other line of demarcation that people dream up. However, we know that all too often this is not the case.

The Apostle Paul, throughout his ministry, continually kept the focus of his message on the manifested grace of God. *"Nevertheless, brethren, I have written more boldly to you on some points, as reminding you, **because of the grace given to me by God,** that I might be a minister of Jesus Christ."* (Romans 15:15-16)

The most astounding evidence of the church is not in signs and wonders, but it is obedience to His Word, expressed by love and unity among the body - we are now in a position to experience and manifest His *grace. "And with great power the apostles gave witness to the resurrection of the Lord Jesus. And great grace was upon them all."* (Acts 4:33)

❧ *Ministry* ❧

CHAPTER 10

Stewards of Grace

In many instances of the Old Testament as well as the Gospels, the word "steward" is commonly used. Even in Christ's day every household of distinction seems to have had a steward or "overseer" in charge of their household, and placed as guardians over their possessions and even over their children.

Today the reference point that we would probably be familiar with is a steward on a cruise ship. Each cabin is assigned a person, called a steward, to attend to every

Whatever the call, and for whatever amount of time you serve in that calling, you are to be operating as a steward. ❧

need during the duration of the cruise. They change the linens, refresh your cabin, and in the evening they turn down your bed and place a delicious chocolate on your pillow. They are your connection to enjoying every amenity that the ship has to offer. You can choose to take your meals in your cabin and have your clothes pressed, all by request to your steward.

Now in the Epistles the term steward is largely confined to the ministry of the gospel. In 1 Corinthians 4:1-2, Paul and his fellow-laborers regarded themselves as stewards of the mysteries of God. Titus 1:7 says that a bishop or overseer is to minister as a steward.

One of the greatest teachings of both the Apostle Peter as well as the Apostle Paul was the message of stewardship. In 1 Peter 4:10 Peter refers to New Testament believers and members of the early church, *"As good stewards of the manifold grace of God."* This is not an option. The early church was commissioned to become stewards of grace. Whatever the call, and for whatever length of time you serve in that calling, you are to be operating as a steward.

Most Christians today think of stewardship only in relationship to money, but what is being referred to here is "serving and ministering to one another."

One area that I remember most from my child-hood was the attitude of stewardship that prevailed in the church, especially in the life of my mother. Her whole attitude was one of service to the Lord and she was always ministering to someone in need. I know that when she gets to heaven there will be many people there as a result of her stewardship.

For many years our family traveled as evangelists, going from church to church, literally depending upon God for food and shelter. It was truly a life of faith, and at that time I wouldn't have traded places with anyone. God never let us down and the supernatural provisions that we experienced could fill another book.

One summer we were traveling through Northern Michigan, where we had ministered in almost every little town. The churches were so magnanimous that many of the people had become like family. One beautiful day as we drove, enjoying the scenery, the car suddenly jerked violently to the side. Pulling a 30-foot travel trailer was quite a feat under the best of conditions, and at that moment it felt like the bottom dropped out of the left side of that trailer.

We had no idea what was happening, but we quickly turned our attention to finding a place to pull everything over and assess the damage. Immediately I yelled, "Pray, everybody pray." There seemed to be no place to pull this big rig over, when just around the bend we saw a clearing and an old service station. We began to clap our hands and yell, "Thank You, Jesus."

When the damage was assessed, the owner of the station said that the axle on our trailer was broken. It was noontime and there was no restaurant in sight. I said, "No problem, we will just move into the trailer while you do the welding and I will prepare some lunch."

He said, "Oh, no, lady, you can't do that because that's too dangerous. In fact, you need to move clear away from this whole rig." There I was with a four year old and two babies, on the side of the road, nothing to eat, and not even a place to sit.

Within just a few short minutes my four-year-old daughter, Marvelyne, said, "Mommy, look at those children." I looked up and I could see a beautiful house in the distance and walking across the meadow were several children holding hands. As the kids got close, Marvelyne insisted, "Mommy we know those kids."

The young boy approached us and asked, "Hey, aren't you the evangelist?" The kids began to tell us that they lived in the house across the meadow. I began to make an inquiry as to who he was and realized that this family had attended meetings that we had held in the area.

I asked him if he would return home and ask his mother to drive over and meet us. He was so excited that he began to run back across that meadow and I knew our prayers had been answered. His mother came, and while our trailer was being repaired we were being hosted in a lovely home by one of God's faithful stewards.

Yes, bad things do happen to good people, but you can testify as David did that he *"never saw the righteous forsaken or His seed begging for bread."* (Psalm 37:25) Yes, we can walk in the favor and blessing of God, in spite of the circumstances, because God's grace is always sufficient.

The gospel of Luke records that Jesus was a steward of the grace of God. *"And the Child grew and became strong in spirit, filled with wisdom; and the grace of God was upon Him."* (Luke 2:40) All through His life, even as a child, Jesus personified the gospel of grace. Everything Jesus accomplished, He did because of grace operating in and through His life.

Requirements of a Steward

Guidelines are spelled out in Titus 1:7-9 as to the requirements of a steward of grace:

*"For a bishop must be blameless, as a **steward of God**, not self-willed, not quick-tempered, not given to wine, not violent, not greedy for money, but **hospitable, a lover of what is good, sober-minded, just, holy, self-controlled, holding fast the faithful word** as he has been taught, that he may be able, by sound doctrine, both to exhort and convict those who contradict."*

A steward is also to be found faithful as presented in 1 Corinthians 4:1-2, *"Let a man so consider us, as servants of Christ and **stewards of the mysteries of God**. Moreover it is required in **stewards that one be found faithful**."*

Paul was speaking of himself as well as others who shared his calling. Continuing on with 1 Peter 4:10, the New International Version Bible sheds more light on Peter's

> **"Each one should use whatever gift he has received to serve others, faithfully administering God's grace in its various forms."**

instruction of how a steward should be equipped. *"Each one should use whatever gift he has received to serve others, faithfully administering God's grace in its various forms."* This scripture says that each of us has been given gifts and we are to minister that gift to one another as faithful stewards.

For many years the church has operated with the pastor or a few choice saints carrying the full load of stewardship; however, according to these scriptures, as a child of God and a member of His body, we are *all stewards of His grace.* Yes, every preacher, teacher, elder, bishop and all believers are *overseers and administrators of God's grace.*

As we can see in 1 Timothy 1:12-15, nothing in the natural qualified Paul to be an effective steward, and he recognized that only by God's grace would he be able to walk in this revelation.

*"And I thank Christ Jesus our Lord who has enabled me, because He counted me faithful, putting me into the ministry, although I was formerly a blasphemer, a persecutor, and an insolent man; but I obtained mercy because I did it ignorantly in unbelief. **And the grace of our Lord was exceedingly abundant**, with faith and love which are in Christ Jesus. This is a faithful saying and worthy of all acceptances, that Christ Jesus came into the world to save sinners, of whom I am chief."*

In this verse we see that Paul is well aware of his past. We also see that he has received a revelation of the abundance of grace, with faith and love in Christ Jesus. This is the key: you will access abundant grace by faith and love in Christ Jesus. This is not exclusive – it's for all believers! Paul makes it very apparent that any success was due to grace operating in and through his life.

It may seem that Paul was a bit braggadocios, but he never bragged about himself. He always uplifted the grace of our Lord and Savior Jesus Christ. You could say that Paul had "bragging rights."

In 1 Corinthians 15:10 he even states that he *"labored more abundantly than they all"* – but he is quick to say that it was the grace of God prevailing in His life and ministry. Even Paul's calling, as an apostle, was by grace; 1Corinthians 12:10 records that Paul received *"apostolic grace."*

Also, Romans 1:5-6 says, *"Through Him **we have received grace and apostleship** for obedience to the faith among all nations for His name, among whom you also are the called of Jesus Christ."*

Profound apostolic grace was evident in the life of Paul and Peter and uniquely manifested to different people in different ways, as evidenced in Galatians 2:8, *"for He who worked effectively in Peter for the apostleship to the circumcised also **worked effectively in me** toward the Gentiles."*

> *All the grace you need is available, and it can multiply, grow and accelerate.* ❦

Two great apostles, gifted, anointed and full of grace; however, each led of the Holy Spirit in his own unique way. There's no comparison here. Read on...

Ephesians 3:6-7: *"that the Gentiles should be fellow heirs, of the same body, and partakers of His promise in Christ through the gospel, of which **I became a minister*** *according to the gift of the grace of God given to me by the effective working of His power."*

Ephesians 3:8: *"To me, who am less than the least of all the saints, this **grace was given**, that I should preach among the Gentiles the unsearchable riches of Christ."*

Paul said, *"My ability to be an apostle came by faith through the grace of God."* All the grace you need is available, and it can multiply, grow and accelerate.

Remember, to operate in the grace you need you must hear from God and receive His guidance, because *"faith can only be exercised where the will of God is known"* and you access the grace you need *"by faith."* This is why Jesus insisted on the disciples and other followers returning to Jerusalem and waiting on the Holy Spirit to manifest. They needed His guidance to follow in faith and to access the grace they would need to carry out the great commission. But why did not all produce the same results as Paul or Peter? Ephesians 4:7 tells us that *"to each one of us grace was given according to the measure of Christ's gift."*

1 Corinthians 12:7-11 says, *"But the manifestation of the Spirit is given to each one for the profit of all: for to one is given the word of wisdom through the Spirit, to another the word of knowledge through the same Spirit, to another faith by the same Spirit, to another gifts of healings by the same Spirit, to another the working of miracles, to another prophecy, to another discerning of spirits, to another different kinds of tongues, to another the interpretation of tongues. But one and the same Spirit works all these things, distributing to each one individually as He wills."*

Grace is distributed in various measures – depending on what God has called you to do and manifested grace gives birth to ALL ministry gifts.

I have witnessed throughout the years many people seeking the gifts and desiring to manifest the supernatural, in order to build a ministry, to gain fame and fortune. I believe that the church has suffered greatly as a result. My heart is chilled when I see men and women claiming to possess certain "giftings." Where is the manifested grace of God?

In the 1970's an evangelist came onto the church scene causing quite a stir. He was in high demand with large crowds and manifesting gifts. Every pastor was clamoring for this man without asking too many questions. I remember as we visited one of the meetings I left very disappointed and truthfully, quite upset. I saw arrogance, I saw manipulation and I saw flagrant misuse of the gifts. I couldn't believe that so many pastors were willing to compromise their integrity to use someone like this. However, I quickly found out that I was in the minority. The sad story is that within a few short years he flamed out, losing his ministry and family, and in the process left a lot of confused and hurt people.

Paul did not lay claim to any of the fruit, but was quick to say, *"He who has saved us and called us with a holy calling, not according to our works, but according to His own purpose and grace which was given to us in Christ Jesus before time began."* (2 Timothy 1:9) Paul was given serving grace to fulfill his ministry properly, and God will grant grace to you to accomplish everything He has called you to do. Hebrews 12:28 says, *"Therefore, since we are receiving a kingdom, which cannot be shaken, let us have grace, by which we may serve God acceptably with reverence and godly fear."*

> *The greatest affirmation of your calling is the grace that operates in and through your life.* ℘

There is no one like you and no one can fulfill your calling like you can. 1 Peter 4:7-11 says, *"And above all things have fervent love for one another, for love will cover a multitude of sins. Be hospitable to one another without grumbling. As each one has received a gift, minister it to one another, as good stewards of the manifold grace of God. If anyone speaks, let him speak as the oracles of God. If anyone ministers, let him do it as with the ability which God supplies, that in all things God may be glorified through Jesus Christ, to whom belong the glory and the dominion forever and ever. Amen."*

Find where God has "graced you" and follow Peter's admonition as a good steward of the manifold grace of God. The greatest affirmation of your calling is the grace that operates in and through your life.

I came up in the church in a time in which people were not taught concerning their "giftings" and "callings" but everything was done by begging people to serve. We just simply filled areas of need with volunteers. We thought that only the preacher had a calling.

We never applied 1 Corinthians 12:28 when it said, *"And God has appointed these in the church: first apostles, second prophets, third teachers, after that miracles, then gifts of healings, **helps**, administrations, varieties of tongues."* There is listed with the other great ministry gifts, *helps*. You mean that "helpers" are called? The Bible says they are!

I am convinced this is why members are often disgruntled and many churches split. Everyone is not gifted to serve in the children's ministry, but hallelujah there are those called to this area as well as many areas of helps and would not be happy anywhere else.

I have known missionaries who joyfully left family, home and financial security to serve in areas of the world that lacked the comforts and safety of the United States. This is what Paul is talking about – GRACE!

Don't lose sight of the definition of grace: *It is **the favor and blessing of God.*** We must be careful that the message of grace has not been adapted to our own agendas and preferences. Nowhere in any writings was the grace (favor of God) used to heap riches upon ourselves. The book of Acts records that the believers of the early church were very liberal to the poor, and dead to this world. What a combination! Not the miracles, not the manifestation of the gifts BUT LIBERALITY! GREAT GRACE WAS UPON THEM ALL!

Matthew Henry's Commentary records:

The beauty of the Lord our God shone upon them, and all their performances: Great grace was upon them all, not only all the apostles, but all the believers, charis megale-- grace that had something great in it (magnificent and very extraordinary) was upon them all.

This is a far cry from boasting that I walk in the favor of God because of my personal possessions. No, it's about me hearing the voice of God, stepping out by faith and accessing all the grace I need for the work He has called me to do.

Proper grace operating and manifesting in and through our lives is mandatory for a truly successful ministry. ✍

I believe that too many times our motives are displaced – we are seeking after things, personally and as a church, that are contradictory to the heart of a steward. Look at the life of Paul. He states in Galatians 1:15-19, *"But when it pleased God, who separated me from my mother's womb and called me **through His grace**."* He states emphatically in 1 Corinthians 15:10, ***"But by the grace of God I am what I am**, and His grace toward me was not in vain; but I labored more abundantly than they all, yet not I, but the **grace of God which was with me**."* Paul makes it very clear that everything he was and everything he accomplished was because of grace. *"No education, no position, put me where I am – only "according to the grace of God."* (1 Corinthians 3:10) Proper grace operating and manifesting in and through our lives is mandatory for a truly successful ministry, and the only way to access the abundance of grace we need is by faith.

If there seems to be a lack of grace, I would ask you to question your call. This seems a contradiction to some because we spell ministry WORK! But listen carefully! No one had it any harder than the early church and the apostles in particular – but what was their testimony? *Great grace was upon them all!*

I can promise you that if you are not in the will of God there will be a lack of grace and the devil will run havoc with your life. Everything you attempt to do will be tedious and unfulfilling; but if you are operating within your call, God has promised that grace will be in abundance.

I am reminded of many people that I have met through the years – some were happy and some were miserable. My friend, your circumstances are not the barometer for your happiness; the grace of God operating in your life and ministry is the barometer.

I believe a key to having the grace for our calling is to realize that everyone doesn't have the same call, and even to the extent that it may look alike but it manifests differently according to grace. Galatians 2:9 opens another window of opportunity for grace when it says, *"and when James, Cephas, and John, who seemed to be pillars, **perceived the grace** that had been given to me, they gave me and Barnabas the right hand of fellowship, that we should go to the Gentiles and they to the circumcised."*

Did you know that grace operating in our lives can be so obvious that others will see it and desire the same grace to be manifest in them? This is quite astounding! In other words, grace manifested in our lives can be clearly visible for others to see. It's on display.

Philippians 1:7 says that, as stewards, grace can be shared: *"just as it is right for me to think this of you all, because I have you in my heart, inasmuch as both in my chains and in the defense and confirmation of the gospel, **you all are partakers with me of grace.**"* In many different scriptures Paul directs our attention to many fellow disciples and followers who were "partakers" of grace. They were blessed by the manifestation of grace in all areas of Paul's life and ministry. His leadership, preaching, teaching and yes, even his suffering. As they observed Paul in good times and bad they knew that he was a steward of God.

I truly believe, as pointed out in so many scriptures, that the greatest need in the church today is GRACE! Grace for the unbeliever – grace for the broken – grace for the forgotten – grace for the lonely – *this is the greatest tool for evangelism there is.* As we truly begin to love and accept one another in the gifting and calling that God has given each of us, and begin to be "stewards and partakers together of that grace" then, and only then, will we shake this world with the gospel of Jesus Christ.